RETURN
TO ME

Entering a right relationship with God

RETURN
TO ME

E. A. JOHNSTON

RETURN TO ME
E. A. Johnston
Copyright © 2007

Published by
GOSPEL FOLIO PRESS
304 Killaly St. W.
Port Colborne, ON, Canada L3K 6A6
1-800-952-2382
www.gospelfolio.com

Scripture taken from the
King James Version, unless otherwise noted.

ISBN: 978-1-897117-50-7

Cover design by Rachel Brooks

Printed in the United States of America.

Dedication

It is with sincere appreciation that I dedicate these studies on the Christian life to

Sam Cairns

publisher of Christian literature, whose wise counsel to man, unswerving faithfulness to the truth of God, and willing heart to proclaim the gospel of Christ through the medium of printed Christian literature is hereby duly recognized.

CONTENTS

Introduction 9

    1.   A Cake Not Turned...13
    2.   The Telling Marks of a Backslider................. 23
    3.   Sin in the Life of the Believer.......................... 31
    4.   Repentance Differs from Confession............ 41
    5.   God's Plumb Line.. 51

PART TWO: Entering a Right Relationship to God........ 57

    6.   Return unto Me..59
    7.   Knowing the Heart of God.............................67
    8.   Guarding the Heart of the Believer................ 77
    9.   Running the Race with Patience..................... 83
    10.   Knowing God His Way.................................... 89
    11.   Hearts Turned to Him..................................... 95
    12.   Hearts on Fire for God.................................. 105

AFTERWORD: Joy and Thanksgiving in the Lord....... 109

Introduction

The first love. When we recall the first time we fell in love with another person certain images come to mind as well as certain feelings describing how we felt: passion, excitement, interest, enjoyment are to name just a few.

I recall the first time I met my wife. I could not wait to be in her presence! She was the most interesting person in the world to me. I wanted to spend time with her, talk to her, show affection to her. Love was in the air! I also recall the first time I fell in love with Jesus. I could not wait to spend time with Him in prayer and devotion. I wanted to get to know Him. I had a passion for God which released itself in service. My Bible was a new book. My heart sang with hymns of praise to Him. My prayer time was one of "wet eyes". His big Father's heart was drawing me into a love relationship that seemed like it would never end. Then... what occurred is best described by a biblical term called *"backsliding"* (Jer. 3:6). What happened? Where did the breach occur? Did I even realize that our intimate relationship was broken? Was I blind to my own condition? Prayer time became a time of duty rather than delight. Bible reading became a chore rather than a supreme pleasure. Worship became routine habit rather than overflowing praise from the heart.

This condition, backsliding, occurs during the Christian journey more than we realize—in fact, often it is only the grace of God that brings us back into a right relationship with Him. What are the tell-tale marks of a believer in a backslidden condition? How does it happen. How can it be prevented? The following chapters will address these issues in a sensitive and penetrating manner. The spiritual condition of the believer is of vital importance to one's effectiveness as a servant of God.

If we have strayed in our heart toward God how can He use us? How can He lead us if we fail to hear his voice because of our wayward condition? The matter of an intimate relationship with the Creator of the universe is of utmost importance in the life of every Christian believer! Time after time in Scripture God has warned his straying people to re-enter a vital love relationship with Him again! Sadly, history has shown how much the people of God have failed Him time and time again in each generation since the wilderness wanderings. It all boils down to our heart's condition toward Him. Are our prayers broken with our heart-cries and tears? Are our hearts burdened with the things of God? Are we living in light of eternity? Do we rise early in the morning to be with Him? These are questions and issues that will be covered in the pages that follow. If you are one who wants to go deeper with God then this book is for you! If we get serious with God He will get serious with us. Let us press on...

Repentance by God's people is our only hope for any future for this generation. I believe three things characterize this urgency today:

1. *The incredible sin in God's people, with little sign that they understand the seriousness of sin. Which is a terrible loss of the fear of God, and this has historically always been fatal.*
2. *An emerging, and possibly fatal, ignorance of Scripture and a consequent turning to the books written by man—God's people, therefore, are turning to the reasoning of man rather than to the clear revelation of God.*
3. *The much needed spiritual "politicians" in the place of spiritual "statesmen." We desperately need men of integrity and spiritual power before God and men. When leaders depart from an intimacy with God, the people soon follow this departure.*

Dr. Henry Blackaby

1
A Cake Not Turned

When the people of God depart from following God; when the people of God fail to obey the commands of God; when the people of God cease to pursue, love, and worship God with an overflowing heart of thankfulness—then they fall into a condition of spiritual sickness which the Bible calls *"backsliding"*. Some illustrations of this are found in the following passages:

"Why then is this people of Jerusalem slidden back by a perpetual backsliding? They hold fast deceit, they refuse to return. I hearkened and heard, but they spake not aright: no man repented him of his wickedness, saying, What have I done? every one turned to his course, as the horse rusheth into the battle" (Jer. 8:5-6).

"The ox knoweth his owner, and the ass his master's crib: but Israel doth not know, my people doth not consider. Ah sinful nation, a people laden with iniquity, a seed of evildoers, children that are corrupters: they have forsaken the LORD, they have provoked the Holy One of Israel unto anger, they are gone away backward" (Isa. 1:3-4).

"The backslider in heart shall be filled with his own ways" (Prov. 14:14a).

All of the aforementioned passages describe in sad detail how the people of God become a drifting people filled with their own plans and desires. There is an even better picture of a backslider in Scripture and this picture illustrates most perfectly what is the true spiritual condition of those who have drifted away from God. This vivid and startling illustration is found in the book of Hosea:

"Ephraim, he hath mixed himself among the people; Ephraim is a cake not turned. Strangers have devoured his strength, and he knoweth it not: yea, gray hairs are here and there upon him, yet he knoweth not" (Hos. 7:8-9).

What the above passage illustrates is the sad condition of a backslider. Away from God, senseless to his condition, he is a *"cake not turned"*; i.e. he is a cake that is burned on the bottom and because the cake is not turned over it is not visible to the eye. This describes the spiritual condition of the people of Israel who had drifted away from God in their hearts (though outwardly still maintained a level of formal worship) and their declension was completely hidden from their perception. They were backsliders and did not know it! How true this is! When a child of God is in a backslidden condition he or she is the last to know!

The process of this drift away from God is similar to baking a cake. It happens in stages. In baking first one needs a mixing bowl; then the ingredients, then the implements to mix the batter; then the oven to bake the cake in. In the spiritual life first there is a mixing bowl (the heart); then the ingredients (sin, the world, and the devil); then the instruments to give sin a reality or opportunity (the mind, the lips, the body); then there is the oven (of God's judgment).

Often when a believer begins to drift away from the heart of God it is usually a **slow process** that accumulates in stages until it is too late. A person who is in a backslidden state can easily and suddenly fall into gross sin without care or conscience. The dullness to spiritual things occurs over time like rainwater eroding a ditch— at first there is little evidence of the erosion then, if left alone, soon there is a gaping hole full of mud. This happened to King David. If one thinks that King David just suddenly fell into a gross sin with Bathsheba on a whim then there should be cause for alarm for all of us! No, no, no. If you study the passage of this sad chapter in the life of this godly king (in chapter eleven of 2 Samuel) you will find that his drift had already occurred. We read in verse one:

"And it came to pass, after the year was expired, at the time when kings go forth to battle, that David sent Joab, and his servants with him, and all Israel; and they destroyed the children of Ammon, and besieged Rabbah. But David tarried still in Jerusalem" (2 Sam. 11:1).

David was not sick in bed. David was sick in soul. His great successes had begun to go to his head. He felt he was too indispensable to go fight the Lord's battles. He was now above all that. A king should rest not fight. He should enjoy the fruits of his spoils and leave the actual fighting to his mighty men. We see this is so in the next verse as he is found upon his bed of ease:

"And it came to pass in an eveningtide, that David arose from off his bed, and walked upon the roof of the king's house: and from the roof he saw a woman washing herself; and the woman was very beautiful to look upon. And David sent and inquired after the woman. And one said, Is not this Bath-sheba, the daughter of Eliam, the wife of Uriah the Hittite? And David sent messengers, and took her; and she came in unto him, and he lay with her; for she was purified from her uncleanness: and she returned unto her house" (vv. 2-4).

There was a progression to David's downfall. It occurred in stages. Much like baking a cake there first had to be a recipe—this one was a recipe for disaster! We see this sad downgrade: he "tarried" at Jerusalem while others fought his battles; he lounged upon his bed of ease enjoying all the privileges and pleasures of being a king; he looked at a naked woman but rather than turning away in embarrassment he lingered, he lusted, he committed adultery first in his heart and then in his mind and then sadly, in his flesh. A well-known preacher once said, "sin always takes you farther than you want to go and leaves you there longer than you want to stay." This was the case with David. For he remains unrepentant in his sins (adultery and murder) for a long time.

15

During this time he still performed his kingly duties in leading the people of Israel and he pretended to still be the man "after God's own heart" (1 Sam. 13:14) on the outside in leading them in corporate worship, but on the inside he was *"a cake not turned"* (Hos. 7:8). He was backslidden and he did not even realize it! It took Nathan the prophet to convict him of his great sins and David's ultimate and broken repentance can be found in Psalm 51. It is there we read his sad lament:

"Have mercy upon me, O God, according to thy lovingkindness: according unto the multitude of thy tender mercies blot out my transgressions. Wash me thoroughly from mine iniquity, and cleanse me from my sin. For I acknowledge my transgressions: and my sin is ever before me. Against thee, thee only, have I sinned, and done this evil in thy sight: that thou mightest be justified when thou speakest, and be clear when thou judgest...Create in me a clean heart, O God; and renew a right spirit within me. Cast me not away from thy presence; and take not thy holy spirit from me. Restore unto me the joy of thy salvation; and uphold me with thy free spirit...The sacrifices of God are a broken spirit: a broken and a contrite heart, O God, thou wilt not despise" (Ps. 51:1-4, 10-12, 17).

The backslider in heart will not love God like he should. The backslider in heart will not be able to diagnose his sick spiritual condition. The backslider in heart will eventually fall into grievous sin. It is only the grace and mercy of God that draws us back unto Himself. But as He draws us back with love we must heed and repent of our wicked ways to avoid terrible judgment and chastisement. King David remained in his unrepentant condition too long, he did not heed God's leadings during this darkened time. It took a prophet of God to wake him up and move him back to the intimate relationship he once enjoyed. After his repentance, King David had to live with the sad **consequences** of his great sin. His kingdom and family were torn from him! May we heed the examples and warnings in Scripture and apply them to our lives as believers, lest we too fall into the same pitfalls and danger. Now, back to our illustration of the *"cake not turned"* (Hos. 7:8). This is the true condition of all backsliders.

Burned on the bottom and completely unaware. Therefore it is imperative that we examine our hearts before God and ask Him to reveal any displeasure He has with us; to reveal through His Holy Spirit any sins that are unconfessed; to grant us the grace to see ourselves as **He sees us.**

When a believer falls into a backslidden state, he or she has no idea of what they look like to God. We tend to think too highly of ourselves. Picture in your mind a lovely garden full of beautiful blooming flowers—this is how we view ourselves. As we enter a right relationship with God we realize that there are some ugly weeds in the garden! We begin to see how wicked our hearts really are. In our backslidden state we saw no blemishes, imperfections, or faults. When God turns the spotlight of the Holy Spirit upon our corrupt hearts, we see not only weeds in the garden but nasty little vermin running around throughout! Entering a right relationship with God will often startle us! Swimming swans soon realize they are ugly ducklings! But we must see ourselves and our sins as **God sees them.** He is holy and He hates sin. Anytime we drift away from Him it is deadly; the longer we drift (as an unmoored boat at sea drifts father away from shore), the farther we get away from God.

The stark reality of facing our backslidden condition can shock us to our very core. It often results in a spiritual crises. But the loving heart of the Father will always take back the prodigal son when the son returns to Him. The Bible clearly states, *"Return unto me, and I will return unto you, saith the LORD of hosts"* (Mal. 3:7).

To enter a right relationship with God—that is an intimate loving relationship, means a **re-aligning** of the spiritual life. All idols must be put away. All sins must be confessed and repented from. Anything or anyone that draws us away from God must be put aside. We must get clean. We must see ourselves as a Holy God sees us. When Jesus was here in His earthly ministry, He said, *"I do always those things that please him* [Father]*"*. Can it be said of us? King David knew how to please God. He was called "a man after God's heart" (1 Sam 13:14). God favoured David with many blessings. God favoured Israel with blessings. But the blessings of God went unacknowledged; in fact, the people of God failed to recognize the Giver of blessings. We see this to be true in the following passage of Scripture:

"For their mother hath played the harlot: she that conceived them hath done shamefully: for she said I will go after my lovers, that give me my bread and my water, my wool and my flax, mine oil and my drink. Therefore, behold, I will hedge up thy way with thorns, and make a wall, that she shall not find her paths. And she shall follow after her lovers, but she shall not overtake them; and she shall seek them, but shall not find them: then shall she say, I will go and return to my first husband; for then was it better with me than now. For she did not know that I gave her corn, and wine, and oil, and multiplied her silver and gold, which they prepared for Baal ... and she went after her lovers, and forgot me, saith the LORD" (Hos. 2:5-8, 13b).

Notice another startling fact in the life of King David, for it applies to all believers. Take your Bible and study the passage of Scripture found in 2 Samuel chapters 5-10. This is a great study for it illustrates how much and how often God had blessed David. In chapter 5 we see how God establishes David as king over Israel. We see in verse four, *"David* [was] *thirty years old when he began to reign,* [and] *he reigned forty years."* He isn't king long until he has his first victory by capturing Zion which became the city of David (Jerusalem). We soon see David prospers, *"and there were yet sons and daughters born to David"* (v. 5:13). God favours David in battles and he defeats the Philistines. We see the most wonderful remark that can ever be made about any follower of God: *"And Nathan said to the king, Go, do all that is in thine heart; for the LORD is with thee"* (2 Sam. 7:3). And then we have the remarkable promise of God to David which details all the many blessings bestowed upon him:

"Now therefore so shalt thou say unto my servant David, Thus saith the LORD of hosts, I took thee from the sheepcote, from following the sheep, to be ruler over my people, over Israel: And I was with

thee withersoever thou wentest, and have cut off all thine enemies out of thy sight, and have made thee a great name, like unto the name of the great men that are in the earth. Moreover I will appoint a place for my people Israel, and will plant them, that they may dwell in a place of their own, and move no more; neither shall the children of wickedness afflict them any more, as beforetime. And as since the time that I commanded judges to be over my people Israel, and have caused thee to rest from all thine enemies. Also the LORD telleth thee that he will make thee a house. And when thy days be fulfilled, and thou shalt sleep with thy fathers, I will set up thy seed after thee, which shall proceed out of thy bowels, and I will establish his kingdom. He shall build an house for my name, and I will establish the throne of his kingdom for ever. I will be his father, and he shall be my son. If he commit iniquity, I will chasten him with the rod of men, and with the stripes of the children of men: But my mercy shall not depart away from him, as I took it from Saul, whom I put away before thee. And thine house and thy kingdom shall be established for ever before thee: thy throne shall be established for ever. According to all these words, and according to all this vision, so did Nathan speak unto David" (2 Sam. 7:8-17).

We must pause here...We must linger here...We must pay attention and take note of **all** the great blessings God had bestowed upon David then and into the future. It is imperative that we comprehend this vital passage of Scripture. God's blessings upon David did not end in chapter seven. In chapter 8, we learn of other military successes and further material prosperity, *"And Joram brought with him vessels of silver, and vessels of gold, and vessels of brass"* (2 Sam. 8:10b). We must take note and record all that the Lord did in the life of David. For it was **after** all of these untold blessings of God **that David sinned**. God was pleased with David up until this point. Then we read with great sadness in chapter 11, *"But the thing that David had done displeased the LORD"* (2 Sam. 11:27).

The divine correlation of God's **love and blessings** toward His people and the sad disconnect of **ingratitude and waywardness** is the black mark on the life of the believer. A believer, once highly favoured of God, who sins wickedly and presumptuously against the Most High violates the blood of Jesus Christ. Therefore, we must do as the writer of Hebrews warns, *"While it is said, Today if ye will hear his voice, harden not your hearts, as in the provocation"* (Heb. 3:15). When we have been blessed abundantly by God and then sin wickedly by overt sin or replacing God with idols then we become useless for any kingdom advancement or involvement in His work. We become like the fruitless vine that is only good for burning. This then is the great and present danger of the backslider.

Because of our self-righteousness we are often blinded to our backslidden condition. Many who think they stand, fall. Take time right now to ask God to examine your own heart to see where you stand with Him. Never mind what you think of yourself—how does He see you? Ask Him now. And remember the promise of Scripture that we each may stand upon:

"Let us therefore come boldly unto the throne of grace, that we may obtain mercy, and find grace to help in time of need" (Heb. 4:16).

In the following chapter we will examine "The Telling Marks of a Backslider".

Vines and trees all require regular pruning if they are able to bear maximum fruit. Pruning, like repentance, involves the elimination of those portions that hinder fruitfulness. A pruned vine or tree doesn't usually look better right after the pruning, but pruning is not done for the sake of appearance. If a vine could speak, it might vehemently protest being stripped of its nicest-appearing branches, but at the time of harvest even the pruned branches must rejoice in the abundance of their fruit.

Richard Owen Roberts

2
The Telling Marks of a Backslider

It is not easy to spot a backslider for most appear quite well on the outside. Not all backsliders are in open, public and overt sin. Many, most, attend church regularly, serve faithfully, and many are even in ministry. The drift away from God goes unnoticed by the one drifting away. Why is this? How does this happen? What are the marks of a backslider?

The very first thing is **lost love**. We lose our first love for God. The sweetness is gone. The passion we once had for Jesus and the pursuit of knowing God all but disappears. It is replaced by activity in the name of Christ; routine service, ritual, intellectual theology, and dead orthodoxy. In other words we continue to be like King David in leading and performing our religious duties but our hearts are far from God. The world is more appealing. Sin is more exciting. The flesh needs more pampering. Self kicks Jesus off the throne of our hearts and we rule. It is so much easier to run things ourselves without having to feel bad about our choices–after all we live under grace don't we? We won't perish for our neglect will we? Once saved always saved, right?

If there is habitual sin in one's life then one must first examine if he or she is truly saved. You may be a unregenerate church member. You like looking like a Christian. It gives you a feeling of superiority to the pagans! Yet you are destined for hell and its eternal torments. There are many passages of Scripture which point to the false professor. The Bible declares that Jesus is Lord. If He is not the Lord of your life then perhaps you may not be in the Book of Life. You may be standing upon a false foundation. The Bible states clearly, *"Follow peace with all men, and holiness, without which no man shall see the Lord"* (Heb. 12:14).

Have you put your trust in Christ? Or have you merely accepted what He did on the cross with your mind? Do you believe in Jesus with your head or with your heart? Is your life different because of Him? Does His Spirit bear witness with your spirit? Is there evidence of your salvation. These are questions which must be asked and answered before anyone can enter a right relationship with God. It is impossible to walk with God if you are lost. It is impossible to live victorious as a believer unless we submit to His Lordship.

We will now examine the marks of the backslidden believer. There are many telling traits that reveal one's walk with God. We will look at these now:

Proverbs tells us that, *"The backslider in heart shall be filled with his own ways"* (Prov. 14:14a). This is certainly true. We must ask ourselves the penetrating questions, "What consumes our attention in life? What has first place in our heart? What gives us our motivation throughout our day?" Let us look first at **money**. What place does money fill in your heart? Is it your money? Where did you get it? How do you spend it? Are you hoarding it? For what purpose? Is money for your own family now and succeeding generations? If God told you to get rid of all of it **would you do it?** Or would you be like the rich young ruler who left Jesus for his wealth. Is money something that stands between you and God? Are you greedy, covetous, stingy? Or do you give freely to the things of God and His kingdom on a regular basis? Do you give Him ten percent and keep ninety percent for yourself? Whose money is it? Yours? Or His?

I have witnessed prosperity kill the life of many believers.

Jesus once held first place in their hearts until they had **money.**
Money then filled all needs.

Let us look now on **time.** How do we spend it? On whom
and what do we spend it upon? The Bible commands us regarding the use of time:

*"See then that ye walk circumspectly, not as fools, but as wise,
Redeeming the time, because the days are evil"* (Eph. 5:15,16).

Do we spend more time watching television or surfing the
internet then we do in prayer? Do we spend more hours on
sports, hobbies, amusements, and entertainment then we do
reading our Bibles? Who is King in our life? Football? Golf?
Shopping? Exercise?

Is reading the Bible tedious to you? Do you find it hard to
pray? Please do the following exercise for this week: take a note-
book and jot down the time you spend in prayer each day. Then
add to that the time you spend reading your Bible each day.
Then record faithfully the actual hours spent on TV, internet,
sports, hobbies, entertainment, family, etc. Get my point?

Have you ever had a love for Scripture? Do you rise early
in the morning to be with your Lord? Do you spend time with
Him throughout each day? How often do you praise His name
each day? Can you honestly say that you still have your *"first
love"* (Rev. 2:4) for Him.

In the Book of Revelation the Lord brings an accusation
against the church of Ephesus, *"Nevertheless I have somewhat
against thee, because thou hast left thy first love"* (Rev. 2:4). Is this
true with you? He loves you. He called you. He saved you. He
poured out His blessings upon your life. Do you love Him still?
Is your love for Him as strong as it was? Can you say that Jesus
is the most wonderful thing in your life right now? Better still,
can He say of you that you love Him more or at least as fer-
vently as you once did? If not, you are backslidden.

The telling marks of a backslider are:

1. Sin no longer shocks you.
2. The world possesses your heart.
3. You are bitter against another person.
4. You complain frequently and grumble about your circumstances in life.
5. You seldom read your Bible.
6. Seldom if ever do you pray—and if you do they are selfish prayers centered around "I", "Me", "us".
7. You care little for those around you perishing and going to hell.
8. You do not support mission endeavors either with your time or finances.
9. Your time and your money are yours to do what you please and to please yourself.
10. The things of God hold little importance in your life.
11. Attending church is a bother.
12. Throughout the day your focus is on everything but God.
13. You continue to repeat the same sins.
14. You have a habitual sin which you keep confessing but never get victory over.
15. You never pray for revival.
16. You are content with watered-down preaching.
17. Your conversation is filled with sports, the world, entertainment, but seldom do you ever speak of God or spiritual things.
18. You continue to have lustful thoughts.
19. You enjoy sexually stimulating entertainment.
20. You have no witness to the world that you are a saved individual.
21. You have ceased to pursue God like the hart after brooks of water.
22. You do not want to know God.
23. You do not want a intimate relationship with God.
24. Jesus is not your Master.
25. You love your sins.

26. There is no delight in church worship.
27. You do not pursue holiness.
28. The most important things to you are your job and family.
29. You are not moved to indignation with the wicked society around you.
30. You are given to fits of anger.
31. You have unforgiveness toward another.
32. You resent certain individuals and they disturb your peace.
33. Someone has offended you and you seethe when you see them.
34. You are comfortable in the world and its amusements.
35. You have little thoughts regarding eternity.
36. Things of an eternal nature do not grip you nor stir you.
37. You have no joy of the Lord.
38. You have a spirit of ingratitude.
39. You care little for advancing the Kingdom of God.
40. You have a lack of love for God.
41. Self is king, you know nothing about the cross in the life of the believer.
42. Your mind is set upon material things. Your thoughts are occupied with things.
43. You are a very prideful person.
44. You tell lies.
45. You are a hypocrite.
46. You are envious of others.
47. You have no taste for spiritual things. You are uncomfortable around real believers.
48. Religion is a chore to you.
49. You do not like to hear the word of God preached.
50. You have no interest in disciple-making.
51. Your prayers are formal and without heat or heart.
52. You have "dry eyes" when you pray.
53. Your heart does not break over the lost condition of others.
54. It is all about you.
55. You have no desire to find out what is on God's heart.
56. You have no desire to go deeper with God.

57. Jesus is welcome as your Saviour—but He is not welcome as your Lord.
58. Your heart has grown cold and callous toward spiritual things.
59. You seldom hear the voice of God.
60. You would rather play golf (or any other hobby) than read your Bible.
61. You have little conscience regarding sin in your life or around you.
62. You are a legalist and a Pharisee.
63. You feel you are above others.
64. You are proud of your academic achievements and feel you are better than others because of them.
65. You have little concern over the plight of starving children in the world.
66. You have behaved badly toward another and feel no remorse.
67. You are full of yourself.
68. You are dissatisfied with your life and you harbor resentment toward God.
69. You have hatred in your heart toward another.
70. Lust easily consumes you.
71. You like to boast and brag about what you have and what you've done.
72. You have an ungrateful heart toward the God who saved you.
73. Your feet are quick to evil.
74. You feel that God does not hear your prayers.
75. You are insensitive to spiritual things.

Nothing is so evil as sin; nothing is evil but sin. As the sufferings of this present time are not worthy to be compared with the glory that shall be revealed in us, so neither the sufferings of this life nor of that to come are worthy to be compared as evil with the evil of sin. No evil is displeasing to God or destructive to man but the evil of sin. Sin is worse than affliction, then death, than Devil, then Hell. Affliction is not so afflictive, death is not so deadly, the Devil not so devilish, Hell not so hellish as sin is. This will help to fill up the charge against its sinfulness, especially as it is contrary to and against the good of man.

John Owen

3
Sin in the Life of the Believer

In this chapter we will study the doctrine of sin and its ramifications in the life of a believer. How deadly sin is! How deceitful it can be! How lasting are its damaging effects! But first we must understand what sin is and know the sinfulness of sin. Few preachers today even preach on the doctrine of sin, consequently many are ignorant on this subject. There is an old saying that "Sin will take you further than you want to go, leave you there longer than you want to stay, and do more damage than you ever know."

First let us look at the biblical definition of *"sin"*:
The Hebrew term for it is: *"taah"* (pronounced taw-aw). It means to: err; to wander; to go astray.
The New Testament (Greek) term for sin is: *"Hamartano"* (pronounced ham-ar-tan-o). It means to miss the mark. A picture of this is when the arrow is shot from the bow and it misses the intended mark. Sin means to miss the mark; to miss what God has for us in life.

Sin is deceitful, sin is destructive, sin is deadly! As believers when we sin we forsake the Good Shepherd for another—self and Satan. When we sin and leave the main path (where Christ is) and follow our own path we err; we miss the mark; we miss the blessings of God upon our life.

Satan, the great deceiver, wants to ruin believers. He wants to side-track us. He wants opportunity before God to accuse us just as he did with Job. Satan wants to throw us off track for the following purposes:

1. To rob God of the glory He deserves.
2. To accuse us before God and to prove to God how unworthy we are of God's blessings.
3. To prevent or hinder us from participating in Kingdom work.
4. To render us useless (sidelined like an injured athlete) for present service.
5. To break our fellowship and walk with God.
6. To hinder our prayer life and render us powerless with God and man.
7. To deaden our spiritual ears so we fail to hear the Holy Spirit's guiding counsel.
8. To make the Bible a closed book before us.
9. To ruin and destroy us and our families.
10. To wreck havoc in every spiritual area of our lives.

These are some of the ways Satan deceives and defeats us through sin. If we fail in this area in our lives we fail everywhere! Therefore, we must be on a continual guard against sin in our lives. Moral failure is the worst kind of failure for a Christian believer. King David had a wonderful life of close companionship with God until he fell morally. Though his sins were finally forgiven he still had to live with the consequences of his sin. We see this through the following passages:

"And the LORD struck the child" (2 Sam. 12:15); *"but being stronger than she*[Tamar], [he] [Amnon] *forced her and lay with her"* (2 Sam. 13:14); *"Strike Amnon! Then kill him"* (2 Sam. 13:28); *"So Absalom stole the hearts of the men of Israel"* (2 Sam. 15:6); *"O Absalom my son, my son!"* (2 Sam. 18:33). These are sad and tragic passages. Many men have ruined their families through grievous personal, presumptuous sin. We will now examine certain types of sin:

1. Reckless sin: sin of passion, sin of lust, sin of desire.
2. Careless sin: sin of ease, sin of pleasure, sin of self-indulgence.
3. Presumptuous sin: knowingly trampling the blood of Jesus Christ.
4. Aggravated sin: sin performed after a great blessing from God. This is the worst kind of sin!
5. Deadly sin: sin against the Holy Spirit.

Any kind of sin is ruinous. All sin must be avoided. There is no such thing as a little sin, for all sin is big in God's eyes. When we sin, we sin before God and heaven. We will now consider ways believer's can sin unwittingly through spiritual deadness. When God has shown us great favour either through hearing anointed preaching or God moving in our lives in a magnificent way and we fail to act upon these blessings in acknowledging Him and obeying Him, we sin. When we quench the Holy Spirit, we sin. When we reject and refuse to act on God's obvious leading in our lives it is sin. When we share in God's glory, we sin foolishly. When we sin against great light, we sin recklessly. The more knowledge we have about spiritual things and the more experience we have as believers, the more heinous sin is in our lives, for we then become unfaithful stewards.

There are many areas in our lives where we can grieve the heart of God through our careless sin. When we take money that God has blessed us with and spend it on ourselves and our families without being sensitive to missions, ministries, and individuals in need, we sin greatly as stewards of His resources. Many believers will stand at the Bema Seat of Christ and shed gushing tears over their great lack of financial stewardship. God did not mean for you to merely stay out of debt with money so you could leave it all to your heirs—rather He meant for you to disperse it for the advancement of His Kingdom. Many ministries suffer because of Christians hoarding their money. Much mission work is hindered by selfish believers unwilling to part with their filthy lucre. Jesus had strong words for those who accumulate assets for selfish purposes. Give careful attention to the following biblical passage:

"And he said unto them, Take heed, and beware of covetousness: for a man's life consisteth not in the abundance of the things which he possesseth. And he spake a parable unto them, saying, The ground of a certain rich man brought forth plentifully: And he thought within himself, saying, What shall I do, because I have no room where to bestow my fruits? And he said, This will I do: I will pull down my barns, and build greater; and there will I bestow all my fruits and my goods. And I will say to my soul, Soul, thou hast much goods laid up for many years; take thine ease, eat, drink, and be merry. But God said unto him, Thou fool, this night thy soul shall be required of thee: then whose shall those things be, which thou hast provided? So is he that layeth up treasure for himself, and is not rich toward God." (Luke 12:15-21).

There are ministries in your city that need your money. There are missionaries who lack and suffer want and experience great trials because they need your money. There are Bible translators that cannot continue their work of getting the gospel into foreign languages because they need your money. Rather, you leave it to your children who will squander it upon themselves when you could have made a difference in the kingdom of God. This is sin.

When we misuse our time it is sin. The Bible is very clear on redeeming the time. When we squander the allotted time that God has given us in life on useless things we sin. Time is a commodity that once spent can never be retrieved. How critically important it is to make good use of our time for God's glory and the good of His people! Many will stand before the one who has eyes like fire (Rev 2:18) and be ashamed of the terrible waste of precious time given by the Lord. This is sin.

Many abuse the temple of God, their physical bodies, through lack of proper eating habits and exercise. Many a useful Christian life has been cut short because of gluttony. Why are so many believers obese? What picture does this portray to the world? Why are there so many fat preachers? Does their message of "self-denial" have power when they look like they have not missed a meal for many years? Gluttony is sin.

34

Many believers are not satisfied with what they have in life. They are unsatisfied with many things. A grievous error many believers are falling into today is cosmetic surgery to improve one's beauty. Reconstructive plastic surgery in the event of disease or accident is a necessary blessing to mankind. When it is used to enhance one's bustline, pull up ones sagging jowls, or tighten or improve other body areas this is a waste of God's resources. This is sin.

Falling into cultural fashions like tattoos on the body is sin. The Bible is clear about not marking up the body (see the Book of Leviticus). When a female believer dresses sensually to entice members of the opposite sex this is sin. Many come to church today looking like they just left a nightclub. When there is no shame in society this is grievous sin.

Telling so-called white lies is sin. Many believers make their children sin by ordering them to tell a visitor at the door that mommy or daddy is not at home. Lying to cover up embarrassment is sin. Any form of lying is sin.

Anger is sin. Losing one's temper is a grievous fault which hurts the heart of God every time it occurs in the life of a believer—who should know better. Anger at another is a terrible offence which Jesus spoke strongly against.

Unconfessed sin is deadly, destructive, and spiritually deadening. A believer should memorize 1 John 1:9 and use this text quickly after falling into sin. We should keep a "clean slate" before God; maintain a clean heart toward God and keep "short accounts" with God in regard to sin. In proverbs we are told to *"Keep* [guard] *thy heart with all diligence; For out of it are the issues of life"* (Prov. 4:23 ASV).

Another biblical word for sin is *"Awah"* (pronounced aw-vaw) and it means to act perversely; to deviate from the proper path. It also means to commit iniquity. When we sin we are behaving perversely and falling off the pathway to God. Once we fall off this path through our sin it is imperative that we return to God as soon as possible. The devil likes to keep us in our sins longer than we want to be in them. God wants us to return to a right relationship with Him immediately! Satan wants us to feel guilty and stay away from God in shame and disgust. But in the Book of Malachi God tells His straying people to *"Return to Me and I will return to you"* (Mal. 3:7). And in the Book of James we read, *"Draw near to God and He will draw near to you"* (Jas. 4:8 NKJV). Quick confession and repentance should be sought immediately when we realize we have sinned and grieved the heart of a Holy God.

Not practicing holiness is a sin. And we have a severe warning that without holiness *"no man shall see the Lord"* (Heb. 12:14b). We are commanded to be holy. Time and time again God commands us to *"Be ye holy; for I am holy"* (1 Pet. 1:16). The following verse of Scripture is a warning that all believers should heed:

"According as he hath chosen us in him before the foundation of the world, that we should be holy and without blame before him in love" (Eph. 1:4).

We must be careful and ever mindful not to harden our hearts against God through sin. Remaining bitter and unforgiving toward another can harden our hearts toward God. Committing a habitual sin can harden our hearts toward God. Remember the verse in Hebrews: *"Harden not your hearts, as in the provocation, in the day of temptation in the wilderness"* (Heb. 3:8). There were approximately ten provocations that the children of Israel committed against God in the wilderness. Let us examine them now:

1) Exodus 14:11 *"And they said unto Moses, Because there were no graves in Egypt, hast thou taken us away to die in the wilderness? wherefore hast thou dealt thus with us, to carry us forth out of Egypt?"*

2) Exodus 15:24 *"And the people murmured against Moses, saying, What shall we drink?"*

3) Exodus 16:3 *"And the children of Israel said unto them, Would to God we had died by the hand of the LORD in the land of Egypt, when we sat by the flesh pots, and when we did eat bread to the full; for ye have brought us forth into this wilderness, to kill this whole assembly with hunger"*

4) Exodus 17:2 *"Wherefore the people did chide with Moses, and said, Give us water that we may drink. And Moses said unto them, Why chide ye with me? wherefore do ye tempt the LORD?"*

5) Exodus 32:1 *"And when the people saw that Moses delayed to come down out of the mount, the people gathered themselves together unto Aaron, and said unto him, Up, make us gods, which shall go before us; for as for this Moses, the man that brought us up out of the land of Egypt, we wot not what is become of him"*

6) Leviticus 10:1 *"And Nadab and Abihu, the sons of Aaron, took either of them his censer, and put fire therein, and put incense thereon, and offered strange fire before the LORD, which he commanded them not."*

7) Numbers 11:1 *"And when the people complained, it displeased the LORD: and the LORD heard it; and his anger was kindled; and the fire of the LORD burnt among them, and consumed them that were in the uttermost parts of the camp."*

8) Numbers 11:4-6 *"And the* [mixed] *multitude that was among them fell a lusting: and the children of Israel also wept again, and said, Who shall give us flesh to eat? We remember the fish, which we did eat in Egypt freely; the cucumbers, and the melons, and the leeks, and the onions, and the garlic: But now our soul is dried away: there is nothing at all, beside this manna, before our eyes."*

9) Numbers 12:1-2 *"And Miriam and Aaron spake against Moses because of the Ethiopian woman whom he had married: for he had married an Ethiopian woman. And they said, Hath the LORD indeed spoken only by Moses? hath he not spoken also by us? And the LORD heard it."*

10) Numbers 13:31-33 *"But the men that went up with him said, We be not able to go up against the people; for they are stronger than we. And they brought up an evil report of the land which they had searched unto the children of Israel, saying, The land, though which we have gone to search it, is a land that eateth up the inhabitants thereof; and all the people that we saw in it are men of great stature. And there we saw the giants, the sons of Anak, which come of the giants: and we were in our own sight as grasshoppers, and so we were in their sight."*

The above examples are for our benefit—for us to view and ponder for our own **safety**. Scripture is replete with such character studies to teach us to forsake sin. Will we listen? Or will we too be like the children of the provocation?

It has often been noticed with wonder by thoroughly orthodox theologians that, whereas many cultured preachers, whose gospel testimony is unimpeachably correct, see few or no converts, some fervent evangelist who does not seem to proclaim nearly so clear a gospel, but who drives home to men and women the truth of their lost condition and vehemently stresses the necessity of repentance, wins souls by the scores or even hundreds, It was so with Sam Joes, with D. L. Moody, with Gyspy Smith, with Billy Sunday. Is not the explanation simply this, that when men truly face their sins in the presence of God, their awakened and alarmed consciences make them quick to respond to the slightest intimation of God's grace to those who seek Him with the whole heart?

H. A. Ironside

4

Repentance Differs from Confession

This is much error in the church today. Many mistakenly and ruinously believe that all they have to do when sin is committed is to confess it and all will be well with God. Yes, it is true that when we confess our sin God does forgive us instantly because of the redemptive and propitiatory work of His dear Son on Calvary's cross. But when we sin if we merely confess it and do not repent (or turn from it) we fool ourselves and grieve the heart of God. How many believers today live in an up and down, walk with God because of clinging to certain pet sins!

Jesus Christ called sinners to repentance with the words, *"Except ye repent, ye shall all likewise perish."* God will not tolerate "pet sins" in the lives of believers. A holy God hates sin and it is His desire for us to hate those sins as well. What is biblical repentance? We will examine this vital subject now. We have the following explanation:

> "First, repentance is not to be confused with *penitence*, though penitence will invariably enter into it. But penitence is simply sorrow for sin ... Second, *penance* is not repentance. Penance is the effort in someway to atone for wrong done. This, man can never do ... What then is repentance? ... it is the Greek word, *metanoia*, which is translated, 'repentance' in our English Bibles, and literally means a change of mind. This

is not simply the acceptance of new ideas in place of old notions. It implies a complete reversal of one's inward attitude ... To repent is to change one's attitude toward self, toward sin, toward God, toward Christ. And this is what God commands."[1]

So we see that biblical repentance is a **turning away from sin**. Not merely sinning, confessing that sin and then repeating the same sin over and over again in a never-ending vicious cycle. Does this lead one to believe in the doctrine of perfection? No. We are all sinners and will be until we come to behold His face in glory in our own state of glorification, when sin no longer taints us. But we can and must be sensitive to sin in our lives for it is an offense to God. He takes it **personally**. In the Book of Hosea we see how God describes a people who are called by His name that carelessly sin:

"For Israel slideth back as a backsliding heifer: now the LORD will feed them as a lamb in a large place. Ephraim is joined to idols: let him alone. Their drink is sour: they have committed whoredom continually...But they like men have transgressed the covenant: there have they dealt treacherously against me" (Hos. 4:16-18; 6:7).

What this text states is that when the people of God sin it is always against God. Our sin is **against Him personally.** And for those of us believers living in the light of the cross and by the mercy of God through grace and the death of His Son, we are held to a higher accountability level than even ancient Israel! We will be ultimately judged by the light we have received. To sin in ignorance is one thing (though it is still wicked before the Lord) but to sin against light given (our Bibles and the blood of Christ) is a heinous act of treachery against our King!

Therefore He says, *"there have they dealt treacherously against me."* The more God blessed His people Israel, the more they sinned against Him! *"As they were increased, so they sinned against*

---

1   H. A. Ironside, <u>Unless You Repent</u>. (Port Colborne: Gospel Folio Press, 1994) 17-19.

me: therefore will I change their glory into shame" (Hos. 4:7). Biblical repentance should be a subject we believers should clearly understand so that the same indictment of God will not be said of us!

Perhaps the great guilt of our wickedness prevents us from coming to God in repentance—we are delaying our return much like the prodigal son delayed his return home to his father. Dear brothers and sisters in Christ please pay attention to this: the big heart of the Father desires our return more than we do! He is waiting eagerly for us to return to Him with a contrite and repentant heart so that He may once again establish us in fellowship and like the prodigal dress us with a fine robe of righteousness and place a royal ring on our finger to show our sonship as heirs to a king! Again let us turn to the wise words of H. A. Ironside on this sensitive subject:

> "He would have His children be imitators of Himself. He brings their sins home to them, thus seeking to arouse the conscience and create a sense of need; for, until they are conscious of sin, there will be no desire for forgiveness, nor true self-judgment.
> "When the guilty one has faced his sin, Jesus adds, 'If he repent, forgive him.' Again, let me stress what so often has come before us in this discussion. There is nothing meritorious in repentance; it is simply the recognition of the true state of affairs. So long as this is ignored, the offender will not seek pardon. When he honestly faces conditions as they are and comes confessing his sin, he is to be forgiven.
> "... how illimitable is the grace that our God waits to lavish on those who come to Him, saying, 'I repent.' There are no bounds to His restoring mercy.
> "Are we not all inclined to limit Him in this? Have we not said in our hearts, if not with our lips, 'I have failed so often. I have sinned so frequently. I am ashamed to come to Him again for forgiveness when I have proven myself so unworthy of His loving favour in the past.' But, if you were to prove yourself worthy, then His forgiveness would not be grace. He

forgives because of the worthiness of Christ. He only
waits for His sinning child to say, 'I repent.'"[2]

The devil loves to keep us in guilt and shame and away
from God in seeking restoration with Him through confession
and repentance. But God is there waiting for us to return. The
sooner we do so the better!

More insight into the doctrine of repentance can be gleaned
from the following comments:

> "Repentance contains as essential elements:
> * A genuine sorrow toward God on account of
>   sin (2 Cor. 7:9-10; Matt. 5:3-4; Ps. 51);
> * An inward repugnance to sin necessarily fol-
>   lowed by the actual forsaking of it (Matt. 3:8;
>   Acts 26:20; Heb. 6:1); and
> * Humble self-surrender to the will and service
>   of God (see Acts 9:6, as well as Scriptures above
>   referred to)."[3]

So we see that "repentance" differs widely from mere "confession". Too often, as believers who sin, we just get to the confession stage and stop short of the repentance stage. God's desire for His children is to forsake sin entirely and cleave and
cling to Him through the power of the Holy Spirit. But for the
believer to progress in the sanctification process where we become more and more like Jesus we must not confuse confession
with repentance.

Bearing this in mind we will go to one more source for defini-
tions and explanations of what true repentance is. We turn now
to the wise writing of Richard Owen Roberts on this subject:

> "The biblical doctrine of repentance hinges on the
> fact that all sin is a grievous affront against God.
> None of us has a right to offend Him. We must turn

---

2   Ironside, 108-109.
3   Merrill F. Unger, <u>The New Unger's Bible Dictionary</u>. (Chicago: Moody Press,
1957) 1073.

from our sin in repentance. Thus it is scarcely surprising that in a time of deep moral and spiritual decline, the world cares as little for the doctrine of repentance as it does for negative statements about sin. It is time for alarm, however, when the church that the Lord Jesus Christ established knows scarcely any more about repentance than does the sin-loving world. Tragically, that is the situation today. Granted, the word *repentance* is still in our religious vocabulary, but it is nonetheless a tragically misunderstood and carelessly disregarded term.

"There are a number of reasons why the doctrine of repentance is so largely neglected and is having relatively little impact upon church and society.

"First, there is a general disregard for biblical doctrine in the church. It is common to hear religious leaders say, 'You must not preach doctrine! It is divisive! The great hindrance to the growth of Christianity in today's world is the lack of unity among Christians. Stress on doctrine adds to this disunity.' How valid is such a statement? It is certainly true that doctrinal preaching is divisive. Preaching the great doctrines of the Bible divides the sheep from the goats. Without careful, searching, doctrinal preaching the church becomes an assorted lot of flesh and spirit that is nearly impossible to effectively pastor. A mixture of sheep and goats are a shepherd's nightmare.

"Further, the world cannot believe in Christ because it cannot believe in the mixed multitude that calls itself Christian. It has no means whatsoever of distinguishing between the sheep of Christ's flock and the goats of the world that sit side by side in the same sanctuaries and mouth the same religious jargon.

"The sobering truth is that the greatest hindrance to the growth of Christianity in today's world is the absence of the manifest presence of God from the church. The Lord has been so deeply grieved by the refusal of the church to faithfully proclaim the whole counsel of His Word in the power of the Holy Spirit that He has largely withdrawn from the church and left her to her own devices. The heart cry of God is most certainly, *'Return to Me, and I will return to you'* (Mal. 3:7).

"Second, portions of the church that still believe in doctrinal preaching have allowed themselves to become grievously negligent about the doctrine of repentance. Many who sincerely believe repentance is necessary have simply failed to give the doctrine its rightful place. They have sought to make converts who neither understand nor practice biblical repentance. Thus the strength of these churches is diluted by unrepentant and unconverted persons in the membership who, nonetheless tragically, suppose themselves, 'Christians.' Massive confusion and ineffectiveness are the result.

"Third, there is an increasing common failure in the church in understanding the mandatory nature of repentance. Some seem to be of the persuasion that repentance is an option. 'One can repent,' they say, 'and maybe even should, but it certainly isn't mandatory.' In consequence, multitudes have sought to turn to Christ without ever turning from their sins. Thus it is becoming increasingly difficult, if not impossible, to distinguish the church from the world.

"Fourth, others have developed the preceding error into a pernicious doctrine that is being widely taught and preached. This grievously erroneous viewpoint insists that repentance has nothing whatsoever to do with salvation. Repentance is described by these false teachers as a 'work.' They insist, 'We are not saved by works. We are saved by faith alone.' Their error is not so much in stressing salvation by faith alone as it is in failing to understand the irrevocable link that always exists between repentance and faith. To assume that sinners can turn to the Righteous One without turning from their own unrighteousness is the height of theological nonsense. In attempting to describe repentance as a 'work,' these teachers are much more successful in proving their ignorance of the Holy One. Sad to say, this grievous error is responsible for incredible damage throughout major portions of the church.

"Fifth, repentance has been neglected because of a grievously distorted focus upon the positive. There is a widespread notion that Christianity must always be stated in positive terms. Some have gone so far as to say, 'If you can't say something positive, don't say anything at all.' Faith is perceived as positive whereas repentance, by such reckoning, obviously falls into the category of negative. But how would you like to take your automobile to a mechanic who always had a positive outlook and could never bring himself to find anything wrong with your vehicle? Or can you imagine retaining as your medical doctor a man who never finds anything wrong with you but always treats you as if you are completely healthy?

"Sixth, the doctrine of repentance has suffered at the hands of the church's large-scale commitment to success. Massive numbers of church leaders have a great love for and commitment to ministerial success. Their tendency is to pick and choose the elements of both religious truth and pop psychology that will most readily facilitate the accomplishment of their purpose. A focus on the love of God, the role of faith in human happiness, the benefits of holistic living and the upbeat elements of a well integrated human personality, are seen as much more helpful in building large churches than thundering against sin, insisting upon repentance, and issuing warnings about judgment and hell. Consequently, there is a noticeable absence of any vital ministry of the Holy Spirit in these churches. Millions of churchgoers have no idea that they need to repent because in their church there is an acute lack of that great work of the Spirit in convincing the world of sin and of righteousness and of judgment to come (John 16:8-11). When there is virtually no conviction, it can hardly be surprising that there is little or no repentance and virtually no true conversions. That the gates of hell will readily prevail against these churches is overlooked.

"Seventh, there exists a tragic lack of moral earnestness among religious leaders. Even in cases where repentance is accurately taught and preached, it is commonly done with such lack of moral energy and vital spiritual concern that few indeed catch the urgency of biblically mandated repentance and respond accordingly.

"How does God feel when His doctrines are set aside? Does He merely smile in the realization that this is a new age in which we live and that the old-fashioned truths are no longer relevant? Or does He rise in indignation against all those who seek to accomplish His purposes in their way instead of His?

"The Bible provides evidence that God is against all those who stray from His ancient paths. It is not merely that God weeps over His wayward church; He stands against it and refuses to bless any and all who violate His will, His way, and His Word. In profoundly moving words Isaiah describes wayward Israel, saying, *"But they rebelled and grieved His Holy Spirit; therefore He turned Himself to become their enemy, he fought against them"* (Isa. 63:10)."[4]

With all of this new knowledge on the issue of confession and repentance dare we miss God and fail to obey His Holy commands to repent? Who among us will harden their hearts? Let us crawl to Him in contriteness with a lowly and repentant heart and re-enter a right relationship with Him!

4   Richard Owen Roberts, Repentance. (Wheaton: Crossway Books, 2002) 16-18.

Modern man has developed the dangerous art of taking the radical teachings of the Lord Jesus and so robbing them of their true meaning that there isn't enough left to make soup for a sick grasshopper. Instead of taking His words literally, we devise sixty theological ways of explaining them away. The result is that there is a vast difference between the Christianity we see about us today and the Christianity of the New Testament. Today it means attending church whenever convenient, putting money in the collection, and giving Jesus one's spare evenings. Is that true Christianity? No! True Christianity is a life of radical discipleship, of sacrificial service, of total commitment to the Son of God. It means seeking first the kingdom of God and His righteousness.

William MacDonald

5
God's Plumb Line

What is a plumb line? The American Heritage Dictionary defines it as: "A line from which a weight is suspended to determine verticality or depth."

In the Book of Amos, we see God using a plumb line to set a standard between Himself and His people. We are not to compare ourselves to the world, or for that matter, even other Christians. We are only to align ourselves against the biblical standard set forth by God Himself. He illustrates this in the following vivid passage of Scripture:

"Thus he showed me: and, behold, the Lord stood upon a wall made by a plumbline with a plumbline in his hand. And the Lord said unto me, Amos, what seest thou? And I said, A plumbline. Then said the Lord, Behold, I will set a plumbline in the midst of my people Israel: I will not again pass by them any more" (Amos 7:7-8).

God has a holy standard for His people. Our job is to realign ourselves to it. When we fail to do this, there are dire consequences. We miss untold blessings. We are chastised. We are judged. But when we repent of our wicked ways and return to Him, there is untold blessings awaiting us. Listen to the following passage from 2 Chronicles: *"If my people, which are called by my name, shall humble themselves, and pray, and seek my face, and turn from their wicked ways; then will I hear from heaven, and will forgive their sin, and will heal their land"* (2 Chron. 7:14).

How do we know if our ways are wicked? If indeed they are, how are we to turn from them? Will we know if our ways are wicked by comparing ourselves to an evil society? Will we know if our ways are wicked by comparing ourselves against other believers? Where is our benchmark? If it rests upon people (whether unregenerate or regenerate) we have a poor standard of comparision. Determining our wickedness is deceiving if we try to do so by comparison of others, for we then fall into the pitfalls of relativity. We can say of ourselves as a nation, "We are a nation that has a certain amount of religious activity in the name of God and therefore we are not as wicked as a country that is completely pagan and entrapped in a false religion." By comparison there is a certain degree of truth there. We can also comment, "I am not as bad as my wicked neighbor who is cheating on his wife." There too is a certain element of truth in that statement. However, all of the above comments fall pitiably short as far as worthwhile standards from God's perspective! For He has a standard and that standard is His revelation of Himself through His holy Word. Therefore we should not judge ourselves based on those around us but only on the One who formed us.

When we see God as He really is, we can say with Job, *"I have heard of Thee by the hearing of the ear: but now my eye sees Thee. Wherefore I abhor myself, and repent in dust and ashes"* (Job 42:6). We have no clue as to the wickedness of our heart unless we see God in an elevated position. How can we possibly know the standard He has set for His people if we cannot even behold Him for who He truly is? Our concept of God is far too low and our opinion of ourselves far too inflated! We must be as the prophet Isaiah who beheld God in glory:

"In the year that king Uzziah died I saw also the Lord sitting upon a throne, high and lifted up, and his train filled the temple. Above it stood the seraphims: each one had six wings; with twain he covered his face, and with twain he covered his feet, and with twain he did fly. And one cried unto another, and said, Holy, holy, holy, is the LORD of hosts: the whole earth is full of his glory. And the posts of the door

moved at the voice of him that cried, and the house was filled with smoke. Then said I, Woe is me! for I am undone; because I am a man of unclean lips, and I dwell in the midst of a people of unclean lips: for mine eyes have seen the King, the LORD of hosts" (Isa. 6:1-5).

In the above passage we see that the prophet Isaiah comes face to face with God. As he realizes who God really is, the Creator of the universe who is high and lifted up and to whom the angels cry, *"Holy, holy, holy,"* he then feels the inadequacies of himself (*"I am a man of unclean lips"*) and the people around him (*"I dwell in the midst of a people of unclean lips"*). He now possesses no "puffed-up" image of himself, rather as he is faced with God in all His holiness he cries, *"Woe is me! for I am undone."* Isaiah has realized the majesty of a Holy God compared to the pitiable creature.

For us to consider the standard which God has set forth for His people we must have that very same Isaiah experience (or like Job) and see God for who is really is. Far too often we have our own concocted notions about God that are so miserably flawed we tend to make God more on our level and thereby **diminish** His importance and **increase** ours! Rather we need to see how wretched we truly are and become like the Israelites when confronted with the absolute power and presence of an Almighty God. We see their response from the following Old Testament passage:

"And all the people saw the thunderings, and the lightnings, and the noise of the trumpet, and the mountain smoking: and when the people saw it, they removed, and stood afar off. And they said unto Moses, Speak thou with us, and we will hear: but let not God speak with us, lest we die. And Moses said unto the people, Fear not: for God is come to prove you, and that his fear may be before your faces, that ye sin not. And the people stood afar off, and Moses drew near unto the thick darkness where God was" (Ex. 20:18-21).

The aforementioned passage demonstrates the **proper** relationship between the people of God toward a Holy God. It is a holy fear! Can it be said of North America and Great Britain today that there is a national fear of God in the land? Can it be said of evangelical denominations today that they have an awe, or a fear of God? Can it be said of you as you ponder your own relationship with the Almighty, do you possess a proper sense of awe toward Him? Do you fear Him? Or is He just your dear sweet Abba Father, your loving Daddy, whom you can crawl into His lap anytime you desire? Or worse, is He just your Buddy? Your Pal? Your Faithful Friend ready to meet your needs when you want Him to? Where is your sense of your own wickedness before Him? Do you feel that you are a hell-deserving sinner who is only the recipient of divine grace? Or are you on the same level as God? These are extremely critical questions that must be answered for us to comprehend the standard that God has set forth for His people to obey.

God has set a plumb line to determine the depth of our walk with Him. It is **His standard,** not the worlds or ours. We must re-align ourselves to it lest we die! As believers we must know God and His attributes; we must seek Him and pursue Him like the *"hart after the water brook."* We must ask God to reveal His character to us; we must plead with Him for the gift of repentance so that we have the grace necessary to do so! Repentance is not an action of the "head" but rather an activity of the "heart". For us to realize our waywardness, for us to discover that we have been backsliders, for us to perceive ourselves as God perceives us, we **must** enter a proper relationship with Him! To do otherwise is deadly, foolhardy, and perilous! We are clay; He is Creator. We are dust; He is our Maker. He is the First Cause of the universe. He hung the stars. He formed the boundaries of the sea. Let us peer into His heart and mind from the following passage that describes our very topic:

"Then the LORD answered Job out of the whirlwind, and said, Who is this that darkeneth counsel by words without knowledge? Gird up now thy loins like a man; for I will demand of thee, and answer thou me. Where wast thou when I laid the foundations of the earth? declare, if thou hast understanding. Who hath laid the measures thereof, if

thou knowest? or who hath stretched the line upon it? Whereupon are the foundations thereof fastened? or who laid the corner stone thereof; When the morning stars sang together, and all the sons of God shouted for joy? Or who shut up the sea with doors, when it broke forth, as if it had issued out of the womb? When I made the cloud the garment thereof, and thick darkness a swaddlingband for it, And broke up for it my decreed place, and set bars and doors, And said, Hitherto shalt thou come, but no further: and here shall thy proud waves be stayed? Hast thou commanded the morning since thy days: and caused the dayspring to know his place; That it might take hold of the ends of the earth, that the wicked might be shaken out of it? It is turned as clay to the seal; and they stand as a garment. And from the wicked their light is witholden, and the high arm shall be broken. Hast thou entered into the springs of the sea? or hast thou walked in the search of the depth? Have the gates of death been opened unto thee? or hast thou seen the doors of the shadow of death? Hast thou perceived the breadth of the earth? declare if thou knowest it all. Where is the way where light dwelleth? and as for darkness, where is the place thereof, That thou shouldest take it to the bound thereof, and that thou should-est know the paths to the house thereof? Knowest thou it, because thou wast then born? or because the number of thy days is great? Hast thou entered into the treasures of the snow? or hast thou seen the treasures of the hail, Which I have reserved against the time of trouble, against the day of battle and war? By what way is the light parted, which scat-tereth the east wind upon the earth? Who hath divided a watercourse for the overflowing of waters, or a way for the lightning of thunder; To cause it to rain on the earth, where no man is; on the wilderness, wherein there is no man; To satisfy the desolate and waste ground; and to cause the bud of the tender herb to spring forth?" (Job 38:1-27).

It would do you well to read the full content of chapters 38-42 of the Book of Job to weigh and ponder the magnificent comments of God about Himself. Finally, after hearing the voice of God speak all these wondrous things to him, we have the answer of Job to God:

"Then Job answered the LORD, and said, Behold, I am vile; what shall I answer thee? I will lay hand upon my mouth. Once have I

spoken; but I will not answer: yea, twice; but I will proceed no further. Then answered the LORD unto Job out of the whirlwind, and said, Gird up thy loins now like a man: I will demand of thee, and declare thou unto me" (Job 40:3-7).

As believers we must **all** come to the place of Job's acknowledgment of God as Supreme Being and Creator of all things and ourselves as unworthy objects of His grace and mercy. Are you there? Will you get there?

PART TWO:

Entering a Right Relationship to God

In Israel, the rain of heaven was withheld from fields and vineyards. In the church, God's fructifying blessing is withheld from the sown seed, which is the Word of God. Why? In both cases, the answer is the same... sin in the hearts of God's people. let us not seek to shift the blame to present day conditions the hardness of men's hearts, greedy materialism, the international conflict, the moral chaos. Let us face the fact in honesty and humilation The reason for the shut heaven is the sin of God's people.

Dr. Ted S. Rendall

6
Return unto Me

"Return unto me, and I will return unto you, saith the LORD of hosts" (Mal. 3:7b). This chapter is a clear call to all believers. We live in a critical time in history: it has been several generations since we have (as a nation) been so far away from God in our hearts and moral conscience. Back in the eighteenth century in America, in Colonial times, there was a reverence for God in the land. Even men like Benjamin Franklin and Thomas Jefferson who would not call themselves Christians still possessed a respect and acknowledgment of a God of creation. It was not uncommon for a city political leader to call a day of fasting and prayer and repentance because of certain acknowledged judgments of God against them like earthquakes, hurricanes, and other natural disasters.

The average person in America back then, at the very least possessed a certain degree of fear of the living God whether saved or lost! God was still in the land. God was still at the family altar. God was still held in great awe and fear. Today we have lost the fear of God and the shame of sin. Very little shocks us in society for we have been desensitized toward sin by living in the very culture that promotes it. Great wickedness which a Christian would have publicly denounced years ago is now accepted and even indulged in.

When a nation commits national sins against a holy God and allows such acts of anarchy to exist without attempting to lessen them or eliminate them, then the nation stands under judgment from God. Natural calamities and acts of war are agencies from the hand of God whether that is politically correct or not. God Himself has stated clearly in His Word:

"For, lo, I begin to bring evil on the city which is called by my name, and should ye be utterly unpunished?" (Jer. 25:29a). A deist believes that God created the universe but sits back uninvolved and disinterested in regard to its workings. He is the great clock maker but he has nothing to do with the working machinery of the clock as it ticks away on its own devices. A theist believes that God not only created the heavens and the earth but has an active hand in them. There is not a breeze that stirs that does not first pass by His hand. When destruction comes to a city through flood, tornado, earthquake or other natural disaster, it is not an outside event that occurs without God — as if God had no control over it. Rather, the gentle rains come by His gracious hand in blessings, and destructive storms come by His gracious hand in judgment.

We have to look at the history of the church and the rich Christian history of America and Great Britain to see how the people of God responded to such natural calamities. We have records of this which we can turn to from the eighteenth century in both colonial America and Europe of that time. Our focus will be colonial America. In the mid-eighteenth century we have the following statements which illustrate how the people of God viewed divine providence in the affairs of man:

> "Earthquakes the work of God, and tokens of His just displeasure: being a discourse on that subject wherein is given a particular description of this awful event of Providence. And among other things is offer'd a brief account of the natural, instrumental, or secondary causes of these operations in the hands of God. After which, our thoughts are led to Him, as having the highest and principal agency in this stupendous work. By Thomas Prince, A. M. And one of the Pastors of the South Church in Boston. Made public at this time on occasion of the late dreadful earthquake which happen'd on the 18th of Nov., 1755. A reprint of the first of the two sermons on the same subject published in 1727. Boston: Printed and

sold by D. Fowle in Ann-Street and by Z. Fowle in Middle-Street, 1755. "The text of the sermon was Psalm 18:7 *'Then the earth shook and trembled; the foundations also of the hills moved, and were shaken, because He was wroth.'* [Italics added] This sermon is typical of the excellent improvement of natural events which preachers of a wiser and more serious age used to good advantage."[5]

Our nation has slipped so far away from the mind and heart of the Almighty. Many are ignorant today of when and why God moves through disasters like these upon cities and nations. In the Old Testament, Israel was insensitive to the movings of God among His people. They were so stiffnecked they refused to acknowledge His ways even when they were obvious and apparent.

Let us look again at another such example from the history of America back when the fear of God was still in the heart and hearth of this young country:

"Repentance the sure way to escape destruction. Two sermons on Jer. 18:7,8. Preach'd December 21st, on a publick(sic) fast occasioned by the earthquake the night after the Lord's day Octob. 29th. And on the Lord's day, December 24th, 1727. By Joseph Sewall, M. A. Pastor of a church of Christ in Boston. Publish'd with some enlargement ... Boston: Printed for D. Henchman at the corner shop over against the brick meeting-house in Corn-hill, 1727.

"Joseph Sewall was the son of Samuel Sewall, Chief Justice of the Supreme Court of Massachusetts. Joseph was born in Boston on August 15, 1688. He graduated from Harvard in 1707. Mr. Sewall was ordained in 1713 at the Old South Church, Boston, where he served along with Ebenezer Pemberton. Although elected President of Harvard College in 1724, he declined the position because of the unwillingness of his congregation to let him go."[6]

5   Richard Owen Roberts, An Annotated Bibliography of Revival Literature. (Wheaton, 1987) 378.
6   Richard Owen Roberts, Whitefield In Print.(Wheaton, 1988) 572.

The short biography of Rev. Sewall displays that this man was no idiot but rather a highly esteemed and prominent person of Boston during his day. He, like many others, believed that the hand of God was in the affairs of men in chastising judgment and that the people of God should acknowledge that fact and re-align their hearts in repentance toward Him. The general attitude of men and women of God during the early days of America was one of awesome reverence and a holy fear toward a majestic God who displayed an active role in the affairs of mankind. America was founded upon such high and lofty views of God and unfortunately the sad moral decline of America has followed the declension of a high and lofty view of God by not only the unsaved but the people of God. We see this reverence toward God from the following extract:

> "A Solemn warning to the secure world, from the God of terrible majesty. Or, the presumptuous sinner detected, his pleas consider'd and his doom display'd. Being an essay, in which the strong proneness of mankind to entertain a false confidence is proved; the causes and foundations of this delusion open'd and consider'd in a great variety of particulars; the folly, sinfulness and dangerous consequences of such a presumptuous hope expos'd, and directions proposed how to obtain that Scriptural and rational hope, which maketh not ashamed. In a discourse from Deut. 29: 19, 20, 21. By Gilbert Tennent, M. A. Minister of the Gospel at New Brunswick, New Jersey. Boston. New-England: Printed by S. Kneeland and T. Green, for D. Henchman in Cornhill, 1735."[7]

Gilbert Tennent was the son of the founder of Princeton University, William Tennent. Some of the most prominent citizens of early America felt strongly about the necessity to humble oneself before an Almighty God in order to receive His blessings. Again we see this from the following:

> "The duty of parents to pray for their children, opened & applyed(sic) in a sermon, preached, May 19,

---

7   Roberts, <u>Whitefield In Print</u>, 610.

1703. Which day was set apart by one of the churches in Boston, New-England, humbly to seek unto God by prayer with fasting for the rising generation. By Increase Mather. Boston: Printed by B. Green and J. Allen, sold at the Book-sellers Shops, 1703.

"Ichabod. Or, a discourse shewing what cause there is to fear that the glory of the Lord, is departing from New-England. Delivered in two sermons. By Increase Mather...1702."[8]

Need one be reminded that it was during the eighteenth century in New England that God displayed His manifest presence through the Great Awakening whereby untold thousands were converted and swept into the Kingdom of God under men like Jonathan Edwards, George Whitefield, and others. There was no fear of man and being "politically correct" back then. Rather, the people of God feared God and submitted to Him. Today the people of God fear **man** and submit to the pagan culture of society. Is it no wonder there is no revival today? Is there no wonder there is powerless preaching today? Is there no wonder that the church looks just like the world? Meanwhile the gates of hell prevail against the church in America today because the people of God lack vision. *"Where there is no vision, the people perish."* (Prov. 29:18).

It is clear that because of our national sins, we as a nation have grieved the presence of God from us in that there has been no national revival in America since the nineteenth century. Corporately as a church, we have grieved Him away from our sanctuaries and replaced Him with methodologies and programs and entertainment. Personally we have lost the presence of God in our preaching and prayer life because we maintain such a low view of Him and consequently allow sin in our lives that should never be there. Is there no wonder that the world sees the church of today in the West as a great impotent hypocrisy?

Can an entire nation turn to God in repentance? Has this

---

8   Roberts, <u>An Annotated Bibliography of Revival Literature</u>, 310.

ever happened before in history? Can judgment from God be halted if a nation turns to Him? Let us look at a biblical example of this very thing. We will turn in our bibles to the Book of Jonah. Many are familiar with the story of the runaway prophet Jonah. He disobeyed God by not going to Nineveh to proclaim this message from God: *"Arise, go to Nineveh, that great city, and cry against it; for their wickedness is come up before me"* (Jonah 1:2). But instead of obeying God's command we see that, *"Jonah rose up to flee unto Tarshish from the presence of the LORD, and went down to Joppa"* (Jonah 1:3). As Jonah realizes his error through the judgment and mercy of God (by being swallowed by a great fish and then delivered from it), he finally preaches the God-intended message to the people of Nineveh. The message was, *"yet forty days, and Ninveh shall be overthrown"* (3:4b). It is critically important to observe how the pagan people of this great city responded to the cry of the prophet. They could have ridiculed him and thrown him out of town which would have resulted in God destroying them and their city. Or they could have simply ignored him as Israel ignored the many prophets sent by God to her. Rather, they listened. The message disturbed them, it shook them to their core. We see from the following passage their response to the preaching of Jonah:

"So the people of Nineveh believed God, and proclaimed a fast, and put on sackcloth, from the greatest of them even to the least of them. For word came unto the king of Nineveh, and he arose from his throne, and he laid his robe from him, and covered him with sackcloth, and sat in ashes. And he caused it to be proclaimed and published through Nineveh by the decree of the king and his nobles, saying, Let neither man nor beast, herd nor flock, taste any thing: let them not feed, nor drink water: But let man and beast be covered with sackcloth, and cry mightily unto God: yea, let them turn every one from his evil way, and from the violence that is in their hands. Who can tell if God will turn and repent, and turn away from his fierce anger, that we perish not? And God saw their works, that they turned from their evil way; and God repented of the evil, that he had said that he would do unto them; and he did it not" (Jonah 3:5-10).

Notice three things the people of Nineveh did:
1. They believed God (v. 5)
2. They humiliated and humbled themselves before God (v. 5)
3. They cried unto God and turned (repented) from their evil way (v. 8)

These actions both inward and outward by the people of Nineveh moved the heart of God and He relented from bringing evil upon them. He spared the city because of their seeking Him in national repentance. God's wrath was restrained. But notice this: the generation that repented and turned to God died off and the next generation did wickedly in the sight of God and was ultimately destroyed. A hundred years passed since the preaching of Jonah and Nineveh fell into greivous sin which mocked the mercy God had given in grace before. Then in the Book of Nahum we read that, *"His fury is poured out like fire"* (1:6). The point is that a country or nation or city that is under the judgment of God can indeed stop His judgment by national and corporate repentance. America and Great Britain today are under the chastising hand of God for their wicked ways and will remain that way until contrite hearts turn to God in repentance.

If you believe this has never happened in America you are misinformed. This country used to humble itself before God as in the following historical record:

> "A Discourse delivered in the first Presbyterian Church of Philadelphia, on Wednesday, May 9th, 1798, recommended by the President of the United States to be observed as a day of fasting, humiliation, and prayer, throughout the United States of America. Philadelphia: James Watters & Co., 1798."[9]

Today, how desperately this nation needs to repent before the Lord to receive the blessings of God and the "plentiful effusions of Divine Grace" which He has graciously bestowed upon this once great land in times past. Who will turn from their wicked ways to seek the Lord of Glory?

---

9   Roberts, <u>Whitefield In Print</u>, 119.

*The Sunday was October 10 ... my birthday ... and
as I preached in the morning, you could feel the Spirit coming on the congregation. In the evening down
He came. I shall never forget it. He came upon a
young girl, Kufase by name, who had fasted for three
days under conviction that she was not ready for the
Lord's coming. As she prayed she broke down crying, and within five minutes the whole congregation
were on their faces crying to God. Like lightning and
thunder the power came down. I had never seen this,
even in the Welsh Revival. I had only heard about
it with Finney and others. Heaven had opened, and
there was no room to contain the blessings... This
went on for six days and people began to confess
their sins and come free as the Holy Spirit brought
them through. They had forgiveness of sins, and met
the Saviour as only the Holy Spirit can reveal Him.
Everyone who came near would go under the power
of the Spirit. People stood up to give their testimo-
nies, and it was nothing to see twenty-five on their
feet at the same time.*

Rees Howells

7
Knowing the
Heart of God

What is the most important thing you can do as a believer? Is it to keep perfect church attendance? Is it to maintain a good testimony? Is it witnessing to others about Christ? Obeying God? Being honest? All the aforementioned are necessary and good for believers but the most important thing we can do in our lives here is **to know God**. If we fail to seek the knowledge of God through a close intimate relationship, all our religious activities are just that. How can we witness about God to another if we really don't know God? How can we testify of His grace and mercy if we haven't experienced them on a personal basis? How can we participate in corporate worship of Him if we really don't know Him? Isn't it all formality and outward observances? Our service can even take on a ritual, lifeless form if we are not careful.

Knowing God is the **first thing.** Everything else of our Christian walk is an **overflow and outflow** from this relationship between us and God. Unlike the people of ancient Israel, who had no direct access to God, we, through the work of Jesus Christ on the cross, have plentiful access to the Father. Do we take advantage of this? Sadly, we rarely do. We are content to assemble each week in corporate worship, read our bibles occasionally, pray pitifully short prayers that focus mainly upon us and our needs, meanwhile we fail to enter into a right relationship with the God who created and saved us!

Are we too busy for God? Is He not interesting enough for us? Do we feel He is unapproachable and too concerned with the affairs of the universe to be interested in little old us? Is it even possible to be in His presence? Or can we just hope that our prayers are heard by Him when we offer them up? The truth is **God wants us to be in a hot pursuit of knowing Him**. He demands that the focus of our hearts and lives is God-centered. He desires for us to approach Him daily and enter an intimate relationship with Him. In Scripture the relationship between God and His people is described by God as a bridal relationship—marriage. He is the Bridegroom and we (the church) are the bride. How can we say we are His bride if we don't even know Him well? Would you marry someone you did not know? Yet we pretend to be mature Christians by our "service record"; when God is mainly interested in our **heart**. His love is unconditional toward us; He draws us to Him by His grace. He provided His only dear Son, Jesus Christ, to die on a cruel cross for the substitutionary payment for our sins. Jesus paid it all! He not only died so we may have life, He intercedes between us and the Father as our heavenly mediator. Where is the Holy Spirit in all of this? Why do we neglect Him so? The Holy Spirit is our hotline to heaven. He convicts the world of sin and comforts the saints. He fills us for service and sanctification. When we pray we should do so in the power of the Holy Spirit. When we preach we should do so in the power of the Holy Spirit. Why try to perform Christian activities without His enlistment? We can do much in our strength and efforts for God, but fruit that multiplies and lasts is the life lived under the anointing of the Holy Spirit.

We can grieve the Spirit away by our sinful lifestyle. We can ignore Him as if He does not exist. We can fail to appropriate Him for service. God has given us the Comforter for a reason. When Jesus was here in His earthly ministry, He guided and taught His disciples. Jesus still wants to be an active part in our lives through the Holy Spirit. He wants to teach us, disciple us, make us like Him.

Let us go to the biblical record of those who have gone before us and had a personal encounter. Let us begin with Adam. In the Book of Genesis we find the record of Adam in the garden. Let us turn there now. In chapter three we have the record of the fall of man that is recorded in verses 1-13. Prior to disobeying God (by eating of the tree of life), Adam and Eve experienced a marvelous intimate relationship with their Creator. But now, because of sin, we see that fellowship broken and ruined by sin:

"And they heard the voice of the LORD God walking in the garden in the cool of the day: and Adam and his wife hid themselves from the presence of the LORD God amongst the trees of the garden. And the LORD God called unto Adam, and said unto him, Where art thou? And he said, I heard thy voice in the garden, and I was afraid, because I was naked; and I hid myself. And he said, Who told thee that thou wast naked? Hast thou eaten of the tree, whereof I commanded thee that thou shouldest not eat? And the man said, The woman whom thou gavest to be with me, she gave me of the tree, and I did eat. And the LORD God said unto the woman, What is this that thou hast done? And the woman said, The serpent beguiled me, and I did eat" (Gen. 3:8-13).

Here are some provoking thoughts from the above passage:
1. God was not ignorant of the events that had transpired.
2. God had reasons for questioning the objects of His love.
3. God wanted Adam and Eve to confess their guilt and name their sin of disobedience.

God's approach to Adam and Eve is the same with us today. When we disobey Him through sin, we break fellowship with Him. Often we are unaware that this fellowship is breached. Any sin allowed in the life of the believer will give ground to more heinous sin. Once a foothold is established by the enemy it is harder to break out of it because the entanglement of sin is like a vast web of deception, which enwraps itself around its victims unwittingly. Sin, especially a habitual sin, is a symptom of a grave illness in regard to one's relationship with God. If a

believer is struggling with sin, and not gaining victory, it is because that person's relationship with God is no longer **vital.**

Rather, it is the tell-tale sign of a backslider. That person is deceived. That person may still be in a **head relationship** with God but not a **heart relationship**. Jesus' strong admonitions about the Pharisees should be a clear warning that God is not interested in a **head relationship** with His people. It is easy to fill our time studying theology and doctrine and gaining a more thorough understanding of spiritual things yet remain completely backslidden and out of the will and fellowship of God.

Often this happens to seminary students who attend "cemetery" as it is often called. A young person can enter formal ministerial training full of a vital love relationship with God and actually graduate completely dead to spiritual things. Sound impossible? It is very common. When we replace a **heart relationship** with God with **anything else,** even reading books about Him or any activity whose primary focus is the "head" rather than the "heart", we are on dangerous ground.

This does not mean we should not be students of theology or doctrine of our bibles. We need to have a proper understanding of all of these. But we must be guarded that our increased knowledge does not **replace** our **relationship**. We can study hard and know the Word of God and fail to know the God of the Word. God's primary desire for us is to **know Him**; not know about Him but to **know Him**. It was the cry of the apostle Paul, *"That I may know him, and the power of his resurrection, and the fellowship of his sufferings, being made conformable unto his death"* (Phil. 3:10). It should be our heart-cry as well!

However, we must realize the stern warnings of Scripture that describe how our love relationship with God can be breached. This does not mean we lose our salvation. No. But this does mean that we lose our fellowship and the joy of our salvation! A person living in unconfessed sin is a miserable individual. The most unhappy Christian believer is the one with a sin problem. Listen to what God says about His people when they sin:

"Behold, the LORD's hand is not shortened, that it cannot save; neither his ear heavy, that it cannot hear: But your iniquities have separated between you and your God, and your sins have hid his face from you, that he will not hear" (Isa. 59:1-2).

The dangerous thing about being a backslider is that God states He **will not hear our prayers**. In the New Testament, we have the witness of Peter, *"Likewise, ye husbands, dwell with them according to knowledge, giving honour unto the wife, as unto the weaker vessel, and as being heirs together of the grace of life; that your prayers be not hindered"* (1 Pet. 3:7).

May our heart-cry be like the Psalmist who desperately called out to God in a prayer for restoration. We must study the words of Scripture to find **how to return to God**. We must realize that God desires us to approach Him in **desperation**, as needy individuals wholly dependent upon Him. Often our prayers are weak and lack desperation. Make the following Psalm a point of deep study:

Psalm 80

Give ear, O Shepherd of Israel, thou that leadest Joseph like a flock; thou that dwellest between the cherubims, shine forth.
Before Ephraim and Benjamin and Manasseh stir up thy strength, and come and save us.
Turn us again, O God, and cause thy face to shine; and we shall be saved.
O LORD God of hosts, how long wilt thou be angry against the prayer of thy people?
Thou feedest them with the bread of tears; and givest them tears to drink in great measure.
Thou makest us a strife unto our neighbors: and our enemies laugh among themselves.
Turn us again, O God of hosts, and cause thy face to shine; and we shall be saved.

Thou has brought a vine out of Egypt: thou hast cast out the heathen, and planted it.

Thou preparedst room before it, and didst cause it to take deep root, and it filled the land.

The hills were covered with the shadow of it, and the boughs thereof were like the goodly cedars.

She sent out her boughs unto the sea, and her branches unto the river.

Why hast thou then broken down her hedges, so that all they which pass by the way do pluck her?

The boar out of the wood doth waste it, and the wild beast of the field doth devour it.

Return, we beseech thee, O God of hosts: look down from heaven, and behold, and visit this vine;

And the vineyard which thy right hand hath planted, and the branch that thou madest strong for thyself.

It is burned with fire, it is cut down: they perish at the rebuke of thy countenance.

Let thy hand be upon the man of thy right hand, upon the son of man whom thou madest strong for thyself.

So will not we go back from thee: quicken us, and we will call upon thy name.

Turn us again, O LORD God of hosts, cause thy face to shine; and we shall be saved.

We shall note some interesting statements from the aforementioned text in regard to **turning to God in repentance**. There is a **process** to biblical repentance. If we fail to notice it, we fail everywhere. Let us take note of the following order in repentance:

1) First, there is a cry to God. Always, the first step is for man to repent toward God. In verse one we see: *"Give ear, O Shepherd of Israel."* Truly repentant people offer up prayers and supplications to the Most High.

2) Second, there is an expressed desire by the people of God. Why do the people cry out to God? What is their purpose? Obviously here it is that God has withdrawn His Presence from His people because of their sins. The people realize this disaster and want to repair the breach so they call unto God to, *"Turn us* *again, O God, and cause thy face to shine; and we shall be saved"* (v 3).

3) Third, there is a call to remembrance of what God has performed in past times. The people of God relate how God has delivered and blessed them in past times to how He can do so again if He desires. We see this in the following: *"Thou hast brought a vine out of Egypt: thou hast cast out the heathen, and planted it"* (v. 8). God is a covenant-keeping God and when the people of God remind Him of His promises, it stirs His heart to answer!

4) Fourth, there is a recognition of a breach between the people of God and their Creator. Before revival comes there must be an honest appraisal of the spiritual state of things. We cannot and must not pretend that all is well in Zion when the moral downgrade and spiritual declension in our land is near its lowest ebb. This must be stated to God in clear terms! *"Why hast thou then broken down her hedges, so that all they which pass by the way do pluck her?"* (v. 12).

5) Fifth, we must realize that repentance is a grace which God gives us. True repentance comes from the Lord. Therefore it is imperative that we **ask** Him for it! Notice in verses 18 and 19: *"So will not we go back from thee: quicken us, and we will call upon Thy name. Turn us again, O LORD God of hosts."* The people of God realize their deep need of repentance, so they ask God to give them this grace: *"quicken us"*, *"turn us again"*.

6) Sixth, there is always desperation in the hearts of a repentant people. God wishes us to seek Him in desperation. Seek Him with painstakingness. There is a price and a cost to repentance. The biblical example of repentance is an illustration of a contrite individual wearing sackcloth and sitting in ashes with dust on his head. When Job repented, he did just that: *"I have heard of thee by the hearing of the ear, but now mine eye seeth thee. Wherefore I abhor myself, and repent in dust and ashes"* (Job 42:5-6). In other words Job's repentance was so deep that every area of his person was involved. Job had reached the point of desperation before God. Have you ever been brought to such a place? Have you truly repented or has it been a halfway repentance, of which there is no such thing.

7) Seventh, there is a commitment to prayer by the people of God. When the people of God get serious with Him, then He gets serious with us! We alert God to the fact that we will pray, pray, pray! And we purpose in our hearts to cling to Him in prayer and not let go in the same way that the old patriarch Jacob did. We see how Jacob wrestled with God in prayer in the following passage of Scripture:

"And he rose up that night, and took his two wives, and his two women-servants, and his eleven sons, and passed over the ford Jabbok. And he took them, and sent them over the brook, and sent over that he had. And Jacob was left alone; and there wrestled a man with him until the breaking of the day. And when he saw that he prevailed not against him, he touched the hollow of his thigh; and the hollow of Jacob's thigh was out of joint, as he wrestled with him. And he said, Let me go, for the day breaketh. And he said, I will not let thee go, except thou bless me" (Gen. 32:22-26).

When God sees the seriousness and desperation of His people through their prevailing prayer, then He answers with spectacular blessings! God will **always** hear the prayer of a repentant heart. God delights to see His people seek Him in earnestness. When we pray foolishly or half-heartedly, He does nothing. When we keep pride in our hearts and pray, He does nothing. When we continue to sin willfully and presumptuously and still pray, He does nothing! But when the people of God vividly portray the following picture, He acts wonderfully in answer to prayer:

"If my people, which are called by my name, shall humble themselves, and pray, and seek my face, and turn from their wicked ways; then will I hear from heaven, and will forgive their sin, and will heal their land" (2 Chron. 7:14).

A young man came to D. L. Moody and said, "Mr. Moody, I want to be a Christian; but must I give up the world?"

Moody characteristically replied, "young man, if you live the out-and-out Christian life, the world will soon give you up." If we are popular with the crowd of worldlings, or if we are not penalized in some way for our attachment to Christ, we have good cause to inspect our discipleship.

Dr. J. Sidlow Baxter

8

Guarding the Heart of the Believer

The heart of a person is a wonderful creation. It's ceaseless beating pumps vital life-giving blood through the human body. The arteries can harden with plaque and cause its functioning to cease. When it stops beating, there is death. As long as it is alive and functioning, there is life. So too with the spiritual life. As long as the heart is soft and sensitive toward God, there is vital spiritual life. When the heart is hardened through the deceitfulness of sin, there is death to the spiritual life. We are told to **guard our hearts**. We take physical care of our hearts by proper diet and exercise, so why do we not take spiritual care of our inward heart toward God? The Bible tells us plainly to:

"Keep and guard your heart with all vigilance and above all that you guard, for out of it flow the springs of life" (Prov. 4:23, Amplified Version).

Therefore it is vitally important to guard our hearts against sin and falling away from God in a spiritual declension. The Bible speaks about not hardening the heart. We see this in the Book of Hebrews where a stern warning comes from God:

"Wherefore (as the Holy Ghost saith, Today if ye will hear his voice, Harden not your hearts, as in the provocation, in the day of temptation in the wilderness: When your fathers tempted me, proved me, and saw my works forty years. Wherefore I was grieved with that

*generation, and said, They do always err in their heart; and they have
not known my ways. So I sware in my wrath, They shall not enter into
my rest.) Take heed, brethren, lest there be in any of you an evil heart
of unbelief, in departing from the living God. But exhort one another
daily, while it is called Today; lest any of you be hardened through the
deceitfulness of sin. For we are made partakers of Christ, if we hold
the beginning of our confidence steadfast unto the end; While it is
said, Today if ye will hear his voice, harden not your hearts, as in the
provocation. For some, when they had heard, did provoke: howbeit not
all that came out of Egypt by Moses. But with whom was he grieved
forty years? was it not with them that had sinned, whose carcasses fell
in the wilderness? And to whom sware he that they should not enter
into his rest, but to them that believed not? So we see that they could
not enter in because of unbelief...Again, he limiteth a certain day, saying in David, Today, after so long a time; as it is said, Today if ye will
hear his voice, harden not your hearts. For if Jesus had given them
rest, then would he not afterward have spoken of another day. There
remaineth therefore a rest to the people of God. For he that is entered
into his rest, he also hath ceased from his own works, as God did from
his. Let us labour therefore to enter into that rest, lest any man fall
after the same example of unbelief. For the word of God is quick, and
powerful, and sharper than any two-edged sword, piercing even to the
dividing asunder of soul and spirit, and of the joints and marrow, and
is a discerner of the thoughts and intents of the heart. Neither is there
any creature that is not manifest in his sight: but all things are naked
and opened unto the eyes of him with whom we have to do"* (Heb.
3:7-19; 4:7-13).

It is wise to take a pen or marker and circle in the aforementioned passage the word "heart" as many times as it appears.
The word "heart" or "hearts" appears six times with great emphasis to guard it. The Book of Hebrews is a book of examples: bad examples (the foolish people of Israel who hardened
their hearts against God in the wilderness) and good examples
(found in the great Hall of Faith in chapter 11). We are to read
our Bibles with the intention of learning and applying what we
learn to our lives in our walk with God. If we merely read our
Bibles for the sake of knowledge and do not apply that knowl-

edge in a life of obedience to a Holy God, then we err foolishly.

Why should we as believers guard the heart? Because the heart is the inner area of the spiritual life. All the outflow of man comes from the heart. The heart is very telling of one's spiritual condition. The heart is the great measurer of the believer. We see this to be true from the following New Testament passages:

Jesus spoke often of the heart condition of man. *"For this people's heart is waxed gross, and their ears are dull of hearing, and their eyes they have closed; lest at any time they should see with their eyes, and hear with their ears, and should understand with their heart..."* (Matt. 13:15).

When Jesus was addressing the Pharisees and the scribes from Jerusalem He told them plainly: *"Well hath Isaiah prophesied of you hypocrites, as it is written, This people honoureth me with their lips, but their heart is far from me"* (Mark 7:6). A hypocrite is a believer who looks good on the outside but whose heart is far from God on the inside!

Again we have the dire warnings of a poor heart condition spoken by our Master: *"That which cometh out of the man, that defileth the man. For from within, out of the heart of men, proceed evil thoughts, adulteries, fornications, murders, thefts, covetousness, wickedness, deceit, lasciviousness, an evil eye, blasphemy, pride, foolishness: All these evil things come from within, and defile the man"* (Mark 7:20-23).

Jesus said, *"blessed are the pure in heart"* (Matt. 5:8). Jesus did not look at the outward physical appearance of a man but at the **inward** man: *"And Jesus, perceiving the thought of their heart, took a child, and set him by him"* (Luke 9:47).

God has revealed in His Word how He describes the heart of man: *"The heart is deceitful above all things, and desperately wicked: who can know it?"* (Jer. 17:9). God also tells us very plainly that when He looks at a man it is at the heart: *"I the LORD search the heart, I try the reins, even to give every man according to his ways, and according to the fruit of his doings"* (Jer. 17:10).

God wants **all of our heart.** He is a jealous God and will not share our hearts with sin, flesh, or the world. The mark of a backslider is when the heart begins to give its affections to the world and sin, rather than God. God tells us how He desires our whole heart in affection and obedience to Him:

"Jesus said unto him, Thou shalt love the Lord thy God with all thy heart, and with all thy soul, and with all thy mind. This is the first and great commandment." (Matt. 22:37, 38).

There is clear instruction in how to approach God in revival and it is found in the Book of Joel. There is the pattern that God wants His people to follow in returning to a right relationship with Him. As we read this passage, let us pay close attention to how this Scripture revolves around the hearts of the people of God and how God wants the **entire hearts** of the people to return to Him. We read:

"Therefore also now, saith the LORD, turn ye even to me with all your heart, and with fasting, and with weeping, and with mourning: And rend your heart, and not your garments, and turn unto the LORD your God: for he is gracious and merciful, slow to anger, and of great kindness, and repenteth him of the evil. Who knoweth if he will return and repent, and leave a blessing behind him; even a meat offering and a drink offering unto the LORD your God? Blow the trumpet in Zion, sanctify a fast, call a solemn assembly: Gather the people, sanctify the congregation, assemble the elders, gather the children, and those that suck the breasts: let the bridegroom go forth of his chamber, and the bride out of her closet. Let the priests, the ministers of the LORD, weep between the porch and the altar, and let them say, Spare thy people, O LORD, and give not thine heritage to reproach, that the heathen should rule over them: wherefore should they say among the people, Where is their God? Then will the LORD be jealous for his land, and pity his people" (Joel 2:12-18).

If a nation, or a church, or a people, turned to God in the way mentioned from this passage from Joel, then God **would heal the land!** He would come in mighty revival and pour out His blessings upon mankind. But for the **larger and more national** picture of revival to take place the individual believer must approach God in the **smaller and more personal** picture of a broken and contrite **heart** before God. God wants us to guard our hearts before Him in obedience and love. God demands that our hearts belong to Him! God wants our money, our time, our service, our worship, but most of all He wants our **hearts.**

"The sacrifices of God are a broken spirit: a broken and a contrite heart, O God, thou will not despise" (Ps. 51:17).

Are we there?

The gospel is "the power of God unto salvation to every one that believeth." By salvation is meant much more than deliverance from wrath and perdition, and entrance into Heaven. That is far from being the chief way in which Scripture treats of the subject. The salvation wrought by means of the Gospel brings a soul into life in Christ, a life under His Lordship, a life of victory over sin and everything that is opposed to the will of God, a life by which the individual who has become a subject of the saving grace of God becomes himself a means of using the Gospel in the salvation of others.

W. E. Vine

9
Running the Race
with Patience

The Christian life is compared in the Bible to a race. A race has set rules that must be followed. The runners in the race must not look back as they run lest they stumble and fall out of the race. There is a reward to those that finish well. In this chapter we will focus our attention on the Christian life being described as a race. To a believer, it is not good enough just to **begin good.** We must also **stay good.** And we must be sure to **finish good.** I have known many Christians who started well but because of sin and a hardened heart did not **finish well.** I am sure if you thought about this you too can think of those whom you have known in life who were once vital believers in the cause for Christ but for whatever reason lost their passion for God, their focus on the spiritual race and they finished poorly and even shamefully!

The apostle Paul spoke wisely about competing in this race of life. He knew the hardships of the race, he knew the disappointments in the race, he knew the cost of the race, he also knew of the prize of the race. He tells us, *"Know ye not that they which run in a race run all, but one receiveth the prize? So run, that ye may obtain"* (1 Cor. 9:24).

Many years ago when I was a much younger man I visited the ancient Greek city of Olympia. There I ventured with some other travelers to the very first Olympic stadium where the first Olympic Games were held. This ancient Greek setting can be visited today and it is quite fascinating!

While I was at the Olympic stadium I challenged some other men to a race. We took our places much like the ancient athletes of old and one man shouted "Go!" and we took off down that track to the finish line. I will not reveal who won! But I experienced the great thrill of knowing the history of that stadium and the fact that I was now running there myself!

We have a picture of the Christian race that is found in Hebrews. Let us turn there now.

"Wherefore seeing we also are compassed about with so great a cloud of witnesses, let us lay aside every weight, and the sin which doth so easily beset us, and let us run with patience the race that is set before us, Looking unto Jesus the author and finisher of our faith; who for the joy that was set before him endured the cross, despising the shame, and is set down at the right hand of the throne of God. For consider him that endured such contradiction of sinners against himself, lest ye be wearied and faint in your minds" (Heb. 12:1-3).

This text speaks of a race: a race that is set before us; A race that we must not only run with endurance but one that is to be run with patience. This is not a sprint that is being described, but a marathon. Imagine in your mind a great arena filled with spectators with their gaze set on the action before them — this is the picture presented. Many preach this passage by saying there are no spectators but rather **witnesses** that have gone before us (those mentioned in chapter eleven, "The Hall of Faith") giving us their example to follow. This is an obvious fact. One cannot read Hebrews chapter eleven without seeing that great cloud of witnesses who spent their life for God in sacrifice and finished well in the race. However, in addition to that, we believe that they are **also spectators** of the present race being run by believers. John Owen, whose eight volume commentary on the Book of Hebrews (and whose introduction to that commentary has over 500,000 words!) stated that the *"great cloud of witnesses"* are both examples for us to follow and spectators who are cheering us on now! Who are we to argue with that? William Newell, the great bible expositor of the twentieth century, wrote in his commentary on Hebrews that the *"great cloud of witnesses"* is comprised of both examples and spectators. Even a modern-day commentary by the scholarly Anchor Bible Commentary agrees with the same thoughts that the *"great cloud of witnesses"* is both examples and spectators.

If this is indeed the case, how interesting the race becomes! Those who have deceased loved ones who were believers are cheering us on as we live for Christ! The great figures of the Bible are cheering us on as we run the race with patience! We are to follow their example and not quit the race. Life can be turbulent at times and trials and tribulations can beset us which discourage even the most stout-hearted believer and we at times feel we just want to sit on the sidelines for a while and not compete. But oh dear fellow believer no matter how discouraged you become, no matter how much life trips you up, pick yourself up and **get back in the race**! Keep your eyes upon Jesus the Author and Finisher of our faith. When a competing athlete is running, it is dangerous to look back behind you to see where the other runners are. First, this slows you down, second, it could trip you up! Rather, press on with your eyes fixed on the prize, not looking back at past defeats or encroaching opponents but run with precision, focus and passion! Each time you get discouraged in the race look into the stands and see those who have gone before you! They are crying, "Run! You can do it! Keep on track! We did not give up no matter the difficulties! Do the same —run and finish well!"

Running the race with **patience** is the key to finishing well. That word "patience" in the Greek language is *hupomone* (hoop-om-on-ay) which means: endurance; long suffering; not to succumb under trial. Jesus wants us to run the race that is set before us with patience, not giving up when discouraged, not quitting when under trial. He wants us to run the track of the Christian life with perseverance and patience; never giving up and never giving in! Many of those believers mentioned in

Hebrews chapter eleven suffered great persecution and even were martyred for their faith:

"Who through faith subdued kingdoms, wrought righteousness, obtained promises, stopped the mouths of lions, Quenched the violence of fire, escaped the edge of the sword, out of weakness were made strong, waxed valiant in fight, turned to flight the armies of the aliens. Women received their dead raised to life again: and others were tortured, not accepting deliverance; that they might obtain a better resurrection: And others had trial of cruel mockings and scourgings, yea, moreover of bonds and imprisonment: They were stoned, they were sawn asunder, were tempted, were slain with the sword: they wandered about in sheepskins and goatskins; being destitute, afflicted, tormented; (Of whom the world was not worthy:) they wandered in deserts, and in mountains, and in dens and caves of the earth. And these all, having obtained a good report through faith, received not the promise: God having provided some better thing for us, that they without us should not be made perfect" (Heb. 11:33-40).

It is humbling to read such an account of the faithful who preceded us! But notice all the trials and obstacles these precious ones endured for the sake of God! And we complain and grumble if we have to stay in traffic too long...or another hurts our feelings. Our exhortation to follow Christ is clear from this text, we are to press on no matter what! If our circumstances become dire and our flesh is weary from the trials of life, all we need to do is look at the following verse and realize our plight is not as bad as we think, *"Ye have not yet resisted unto blood, striving against sin"* (Heb. 12:4).

Persecution has not yet come to the Western world but there are many who suffer physically for their faith. Our race is easy compared to many others. Our Master is trying to get us to see that if we get discouraged in the race to look to those who really suffered for their faith; no matter how bad it gets for us, are we "sawn in half" for our faith?

But we must run like the athletes of old who ran unencumbered, for we must cast off things which drag us down and distract us from our spiritual progress. We too must, *"lay aside every weight, and the sin which doth so easily beset us"* (Heb. 12:1). Sin must be avoided at all costs when running the race of the Christian. We need to take the advice of the apostle Paul to his young disciple Timothy: *"Flee also youthful lusts: but follow righteousness, faith, charity, peace, with them that call on the Lord out of a pure heart"* (2 Tim. 2:22). We must also be able to say with Paul toward the end of our race, *"Therefore I endure all things for the elect's sakes, that they may also obtain the salvation which is in Christ Jesus with eternal glory"* (2 Tim. 2:10). And lastly, after we have run well the course which is set before us, we can say with Paul: *"I have fought a good fight, I have finished my course, I have kept the faith"* (2 Tim. 4:7).

The serious problem of our age is that Christian men and women are sinning against the Holy Spirit. The reformer, John Calvin, was right when he pointed out that the sin of Old Testament times was the rejection of Jehovah God, the sin of New Testament times was the rejection of the Son of God, and the sin of the Church age has been the rejection of the Holy Spirit. There are so-called believers all over Christendom today who refuse to acknowledge the sovereignty of the Holy Spirit in individual and congregational life. These people are not living in the fullness and freedom and fellowship of the Spirit. This is why we do not know a contagious revival. But let us not be pessimistic: revival **can** *and* **will** *come, carrying in its wake all the blessings which are promised to us in Christ, if we are prepared to discover the secret, discern the signs and determine the scope of a heaven-sent revival.*

Dr. Stephen F. Olford

10
Knowing God His Way

There is an old story of a man who loved to hear good preachers. This man lived in England during the seventeenth century and he often traveled to Scotland to hear some of the great preachers there. Scotland has been known for a land of great preaching. One such journey, he set out and came to a country parish and he listened to a preacher who showed him the majesty of God. The text was from Isaiah chapter six where the prophet Isaiah was confronted with the terrible majesty of a God who was *"high and lifted up"*. Next the traveler went to a church in the highlands and he was confronted with a preacher who preached on the text from Jeremiah which states, *"The heart is deceitful above all things, and desperately wicked: who can know it?"* (Jer. 17:9). And this man showed him the wickedness of his own heart. Then traveling a little further toward the great Capital of Edinburgh he stopped in a church to hear a man preach on the loveliness of Christ. Notice the order of the three messages for they speak volumes on our relationship with God. It is imperative that this same order be experienced in our own lives. We must come face to face with the following:

1) The Majesty of a Holy God
2) The Wickedness of our Human Heart
3) The Beauty and Loveliness of Jesus Christ

When we get these out of order we miss the proper relationship that God wants us to maintain with Him. If we put our heart first then the emphasis is too much on us and we drift toward humanism and a man-centered theology. If we put first the beauty of Jesus and that is our desire, it can result in a false conversion because we make an intellectual ascent to God and the heart remains unregenerate. But if we proceed from the facts of how God is a high and lifted up God whose name is Holy and who dwells among the cherubim, then we can see sin as He sees it! We can see ourselves as ants compared to Him. We see that there is nothing in us worthwhile for His mercy and grace to be poured upon. Next, if we view our wicked hearts for what they are, this will get rid of the evil of pride in our hearts. It will put us in a right relationship with God. There will be no self-righteousness if we see how desperately wicked our own hearts are and how prone they are to wander away from a Holy God. We will be faced with our hell-deserving sins and realize we are truly sinful wretches in need of a Saviour. Lastly, when we put Jesus as our **remedy** of sin, as our Redeemer from sin, as our Lord and Saviour of our eternal salvation, then we have a proper view of God and what God has done for us. Too often we fail to comprehend any of the above and just focus on ourselves and what Jesus has done for us and we continue to allow wicked sin in our lives which breaks the heart of the God who saved us! We must hate sin as He hates it! We must not tolerate sin in our lives if we are to live a life pleasing to Him. As believers we tend to rely too much on grace and hold onto our sins expecting a place already reserved for us in eternity. While the believer cannot lose his salvation through sin he can lose his rewards in eternity. One cannot work or earn salvation (this is work-based justification which doesn't work!) but one can work toward future rewards.

It is critically important for believers to understand how God views a backsliding people. He will not tolerate a backslider long. When we do not have a proper view of God as high and lifted up, we then put Him on our level and we assume if we can tolerate sin in the world and in our life then He can too! No, no, no. There is a high calling of God for the Christian that we must strive to be found faithful in a holy walk with Him. Listen to the words of the apostle Paul along these lines:

"Not as though I had already attained, either were already perfect: but I follow after, if that I may apprehend that for which also I am apprehended of Christ Jesus. Brethren, I count not myself to have apprehended: but this one thing I do, forgetting those things which are behind, and reaching forth unto those things which are before. I press toward the mark for the prize of the high calling of God in Christ Jesus. Let us therefore, as many as be perfect, be thus minded: and if in any thing ye be otherwise minded, God shall reveal even this unto you. Nevertheless, whereto we have already attained, let us walk by the same rule, let us mind the same thing. Brethren, be followers together of me, and mark them which walk so as ye have us for an example" (Phil. 3:12-17).

Paul knew what it took to live for Christ with victory! He knew the trials, the heartaches, but he also knew the prize which was before him—Jesus and heaven! We should live as Paul with our eyes fixed upon Him; living, working, serving, toward a future in eternity which will never end!

But listen fellow believers! It is so easy to become a backslider. This I know full well from personal experience. When we cease to pursue God with our **hearts** in a passionate love relationship with Him then we replace Him with other things. Our hearts soon grow cold toward Him. We can still assemble ourselves in corporate worship each week, still serve God in some teaching/preaching or witnessing capacity and our hearts can be as far away from Him as night from day. We allow sin in our lives because we **love to have it so.** Please carefully ponder the following text which describes (from God's perspective) a backslidden people:

"Hear now this, O foolish people, and without understanding; which have eyes, and see not; which have ears, and hear not: Fear ye not me? saith the LORD: will ye not tremble at my presence, which have placed the sand for the bound of the sea by a perpetual decree, that it cannot pass it: and though the waves thereof toss themselves, yet can they not prevail; though they roar, yet can they not pass over it? But this people hath a revolting and a rebellious heart; they are revolted

and gone. Neither say they in their heart, Let us now fear the LORD our God, that giveth rain, both the former and the latter, in his season: he reserveth unto us the appointed weeks of the harvest. Your iniquities have turned away these things, and your sins have withholden good things from you. For among my people are found wicked men: they lay wait, as he that setteth snares; they set a trap, they catch men. As a cage is full of birds, so are their houses full of deceit: therefore they are become great, and waxen rich. They are waxen fat, they shine: yea, they overpass the deeds of the wicked: they judge not the cause, the cause of the fatherless, yet they prosper; and the right of the needy do they not judge. Shall I not visit for these things? saith the LORD: shall not my soul be avenged on such a nation as this? A wonderful and horrible thing is committed in the land; The prophets prophesy falsely, and the priests bear rule by their means; and my people love to have it so: and what will ye do in the end thereof?" (Jer. 5:21-31).

Any nation should study this aforementioned text carefully to avoid God's judgment upon them. In these days of desperation, it is time for the people of God to **return to Him.** If we fail to do so, then we deserve the coming catastrophe and judgment. If we fail to turn our hearts toward Him and repent of our sins and seek His face in humility and contriteness then we do so because *"my people love to have it so."*

Revival begins with **you.** How can you lead others to revival if you yourself have not returned to a Holy God as you should? Let it be said of you as Joshua said, *"As for me and my house, we will serve the LORD."*

It is our prayer that you take God at His Word and seek Him in repentance and expectation as to what He can do! His promise remains: *"Return to me and I shall return to you."* Why wait any longer?

Lord engage my heart today
With zeal that will not pass away,
Now torch it with Thy holy fire
That never more shall time's desire
Invade or quench the Heaven born power.
I would be trapped with in Thy holy will,
Thine every holy purpose to fulfil
That every effort of my life shall bring
Rapturous praise to my Eternal King.
I pledge from this day to the grave
To be Thine own unquestioning slave.

The last poem of Leonard Ravenhill

11
Hearts Turned to Him

There is a vast difference between a believer who is luke-warm toward God versus a believer whose heart is hot toward God. Jesus has stern admonition toward believers who are in this pitiable condition. In the Book of Revelation Jesus has this to say to the church of Laodicea:

"I know thy works, that thou art neither cold nor hot: I would thou wert cold or hot. So then because thou art lukewarm, and neither cold nor hot, I will spew thee out of my mouth. Because thou say-est, I am rich, and increased with goods, and have need of nothing; and knowest not that thou art wretched, and miserable, and poor, and blind, and naked: I counsel thee to buy of me gold tried in the fire, that thou mayest be rich; and white raiment, that thou mayest be clothed, and that the shame of thy nakedness do not appear; and anoint thine eyes with eye salve, that thou mayest see. As many as I love, I rebuke and chasten: be zealous therefore, and repent" (Rev. 3:15-19).

Many sermons are preached and many Sunday school les-sons are taught by Christian workers who have let their hearts grow cold toward God. In this "lukewarm" spiritual condition, there is no life nor fruit; their messages are without heart or heat. Few are affected by them yet alone transformed for eter-nity. Is it any wonder the church lacks power today? When its workers are not even in a deepening love relationship with the One who saved them?

It is always obvious when someone is on fire for God. You

can feel the heat by just being around them! Their love for God is contagious. They are like salt—being around them makes you thirsty for Jesus and eternity. We may wonder at Christians like that and mistakenly believe they possess something unattainable by other mortals. Why do they have such influence for God? Why is God using them so dramatically and letting others stay on the sidelines? What makes them tick? The answer is found in two passages of Scripture; one in the Old Testament and the other in the New Testament. We will begin with the Old Testament:

"As the hart panteth after the water brooks, so panteth my soul after thee, O God. My soul thirsteth for God, for the living God: when shall I come and appear before God? My tears have been my meat day and night, while they continually say unto me, Where is thy God? When I remember these things, I pour out my soul in me: for I had gone with the multitude, I went with them to the house of God, with the voice of joy and praise, with a multitude that kept holyday. Why art thou cast down, O my soul? and why art thou disquieted in me? hope thou in God: for I shall yet praise him for the help of his counte-nance" (Ps. 42:1-5).

This passage from Psalms is written by a man who once walked closely with God and who now laments over the broken relationship. He is thirsty for the ways things **were.** He is thirsting for God Himself. He admits his lack of God in his life. He remembers the days when it wasn't so (v.4). When a deer is chased through the forest by an adversary it runs full speed to escape—it is running for its life. When the animal finds itself free from danger it realizes how thirsty it is and it longs, it pants for the water brook to satiate that thirst. When a believer falls out of fellowship with God and he realizes that he is out of danger (of the enemy of his soul), by the providence of God he comes to his senses and thirsts for what was there before—a vital love relationship between he and the Master.

We see something of the same in the New Testament passage which relates to this as well, found in the Gospel of Luke:

"And, behold, two of them went that same day to a village called Emmaus, which was from Jerusalem about threescore furlongs. And they talked together of all these things which had happened. And it came to pass, that, while they communed together and reasoned, Jesus himself drew near, and went with them. But their eyes were holden that they should not know him. And he said unto them, What manner of communications are these that ye have one to another, as ye walk, and are sad? And the one of them, whose names was Cleopas, answering said unto him, Art thou a stranger in Jerusalem, and hast not known the things which are come to pass there in these days? And he said unto them, What things? And they said unto him, Concerning Jesus of Nazareth, which was a prophet mighty in deed and word before God and all the people: And how the chief priests and our rulers delivered him to be condemned to death, and have crucified him. But we trusted that it had been he which should have redeemed Israel: and beside all this, today is the third day since these things were done. Yea, and certain women also of our company made us astonished, which were early at the sepulcher; And when they found not his body, they came, saying, that they had also seen a vision of angels, which said that he was alive. And certain of them which were with us went to the sepulcher, and found it even so as the women had said: but him they saw not. Then he said unto them, O fools, and slow of heart to believe all that the prophets have spoken: Ought not Christ to have suffered these things, and to enter into his glory? And beginning at Moses and all the prophets, he expounded unto them in all the scriptures the things concerning himself. And they drew nigh unto the village, whither they went: and he made as though he would have gone further. But they constrained him, saying, Abide with us: for it is toward evening, and the day is far spent. And he went in to tarry with them. And it came to pass, as he sat at meat with them, he took bread, and blessed it, and broke, and gave to them. And their eyes were opened, and they knew him; and he vanished out of their sight. And they said one to another, Did not our heart burn within us, while he talked with us by the way, and while He opened to us the scriptures?" (Luke 24:13-32).

We can learn much from this New Testament passage: 1) The hearts of the disciples had become discouraged and they had gone out of his fellowship and were downcast in their spirit.

2) Their encounter with Jesus on the road made their hearts burn within them as in former times. 3) They desired more of His company by inviting Him to stay with them. 4) Their lives were never the same again after this encounter.

Is it not so with us when we realize the reason for our downcast soul (our lack of a love relationship with Him) and we hunger to be with Him once more? Once we have this encounter with God we are forever changed! Saul met Jesus on the road of Damascus and he was forever changed to the glory of God! Jacob wrestled with God and was dramatically changed! Moses met God at the burning bush and his life was transformed! It can be the same with us.

People that have been touched by God have a uniqueness to them. They make you desire to be in their presence to discuss spiritual things. They are impassioned believers. They are contagious Christians. Look at the following letter written during the Revival of Religion which took place in the eighteenth century under George Whitefield and John Wesley in England (and eventually Scotland, Wales, Ireland, and the American colonies under George Whitefield and Jonathan Edwards—known as The Great Awakening). The letter is written by Howell Harris who was a co-labourer with George Whitefield and John Wesley. It was written during the revival and shows clearly how God had taken hold of this young Welshman! He was on fire for God! The letter is written in 1741 to a Mr. John Lewis of England who was printing an account of the revival of religion in a weekly paper called "The Weekly History". Here is the letter:

> "Dear Brother Lewis,   March 1741-2
> "In your paper No. 43 I saw an exceeding sweet Letter from *Leominster*, where was most sweet, tender, wholesome, and necessary advice to a young minister, and I was made to admire the love of my dear Lord I taking that kind and tender manner to reprove the person meant there, whoever he was; but also it came home to me, tho' I know I was not intended by the writer: and as I am persuaded it was God's love

made that good man write so from a true concern... As to the first, I know this experimentally; when the Lord Jesus is reveal'd , tho' but in a weak degree, to the Eye of Faith, in his Names, Offices, and Relations, in his active and passive Obedience, in his Divinity and Humanity, in his Humiliation and Exaltation; and when the glorious Deliverances and Privileges that he has purchased for us are a little laid before the Soul's eye by the Holy Spirit, and seeing what are the Fruits of this Light on his own Soul, what Zeal he feels for the Glory of this Jesus, now he knows not what to do first for him, how to spend and be spent all for him.—Had he a Thousand Tongues and Lives they would all be employ'd for him and his Cause. Had he Millions a Year, he wou'd use 'em all for Christ. When in that Light he sees that all the secret Pleasure he takes in looking at fine Houses, fine Dress, fine Ornaments in Houses, &c. is no otherwise than admiring the Devil in his Works of Pride; and when he considers that if he was to forget himself so as to spend some Money on useless (if not vain) Extravagancies, not necessary for a Follower of Jesus Christ, how shou'd he cut his Heart for offering that as a Sacrifice to the Idol Self and the Devil; and not only that, but disenables himself from giving, at least so plentifully, toward carrying on the Work of the Lord; nay, perhaps, some of the Royal Seed of Jesus here in Want while he spent his Money thus on the Lust of the Eye, &c. When also in this Light he sees the Evil of idle Words as being Fruits not from Faith, nor acceptable to God; and carnal Mirth being the Fruits of the Flesh, and all Conformity to the Pride and Fashions and Principles of the World; and when he feels how he loses Fellowship with God in all these, and is cut to the Heart for them, and can no more live in them than in Adultery.—'Tis not to be so much wonder'd then if any one walking in this Light, shou'd severely cut any that indulge themselves in light fruitless Talk, being not the Salt of the Earth—proud, fashionable and modish in their Dress, carnal in their Mirth, without a Zeal bearing Fruit for the Cause of God, and at the same time taking on them the Name of Christian, and talking of separating from the World, tho' not departing from Iniquity; and not sensible too they are decaying and dwindling into a dead Formality; and at bell but asleep, and bearing no Fruit to God, and so dishonour him, but angry at any Attempt to awaken them, calling it judging, persecuting, and pleading for these Things.

If the Scripture did not make mention of the wise Virgins sleeping with the foolish ones, who could have Charity enough to hope that there was any Life at all in our Congregations where there is sweet Talk of Christ?—Who can believe that Heart is right with God, and loves God, and his Name and Interest more than himself and Name, and finds that if you were to set some Cause of God before him, to call for his help to carry it on, it wou'd be with Difficulty he cou'd give you five or ten Pounds, or perhaps less, whereas he cou'd freely layout ten times the Sum, or more, in buying Multitudes of Dress for himself, and Apparel, in being in all the Follies and Madness of the Mode of the Age; and also in furnishing his House with every thing that may please the Lust of the Eye, and may make him admired by his carnal Friends? For there Things are an Abomination and an Offence to his spiritual Friends— Who cou'd in Charity hope that the Power of Godliness is in those Congregations where is so much playing with Children on the Lap, such gazing about, so many dry Eyes, such handing the Snuff-box, such wide Hoops as two or three Ladies almost fill a Seat, such Pomp and Vanity, and such Lukewarmness and Indifferency in delivering and receiving the Oracles of the Holy One of Israel?— Where is the lifting tip of the Voice like a Trumpet?—The bearing an open Testimony against these Conformities, these Backs? Is this taking up our Cross, dying to ourselves and the World, following a despised Jesus? We shall be hated of none thus for his Name's-sake—I fear the Threatning of being spued out of God's Mouth, and the Danger of having the Candlestick removed out of its Place is not missapply'd here, and the Living will lay it to heart, and repent, and do the first Works, and be warned in Time.

I fear that some faithful, but weak Ministers, are

as yet in great Bondage thro' fear of offending their Congregations, or some great Man there, whom they carnally look on as a good Friend to their Cause, &c.—and fear to speak out, and so go Mourning, denying their own Master, by studying to please many, and so grieve the Spirit of God—but God will visit his faithful ones, and set them free, and make them bold as Lions. Then the Devil will rage and there will be Standing between the Dead and the Living; and all that will be alive to and for God, of all Seas, will shake off the carnal drouzy ones that now lull them asleep, and the narrow bigotted ones that now keep them from walking with God's dear ones, who walk with him, of other Opinions, and so robbing them of much Fellowship with the Lord and his dear ones.—Let also the Children of God that may now be asleep , or half awakened, stirr'd up by one Discourse, and lull'd asleep again by the next, consider how fruitless they now are, and what a terrible Consequence attends that—that God is dishonoured, and they cumber the Ground, and they love Fellowship with God, and become useless with all their Talents to the Church of God. These are more terrible to the Soul that is born of God, than all the Threatnings of Mount Sinai are to the natural Man, and will awaken the new Life to Activity if apply'd by the Spirit—As I feel 'tis a Concern for my Lord's Glory; and as there are some in every Sea that are not concerned in this, and some in everyone may peradventure say, *I am the Man.* And as I don't apply, but have been helped all through to speak it to all, without any particular Application to any Sect, or Man, or Men, in particular, it can't be taken to stir up any Spirit but Self-Examination and Humiliation, or as intended to no other use by Poor, Unworthy, Sinful

Howell Harris."[10]

If more believers lived each hour with the same heartbeat for Christ as this dear man from the eighteenth century, we would turn the world upside down for God! We must ask

---

10   J. Lewis, *The Weekly History.* (Quinta Press, 2006) 292-294.

ourselves the penetrating question: "What object has the affections of my heart?" Is it the Lord or the world? If it truly is the Lord who has your heart's affections, then is there outward evidence of this fact? Do people see you as one who is on fire for God? Or are you perceived as just a nominal Christian?

In the evening, singing hymns with friends, my soul
seemed to melt, and in prayer afterwards enjoyed
the exercise of faith and was enabled to be fervent
in spirit. Found more of God's presence than I have
done any time in my late wearisome journey. Eter-
nity appeared very near; my nature was very weak
and seemed ready to be dissolved, the sun declining,
and the shadows of the evening drawing on apace.
Oh, I longed to fill up the remaining moments all
for God! Though my body was so feeble, and wearied
with preaching and much private conversation, yet I
wanted to sit up all night to do something for God.

David Brainerd

12
Hearts on Fire for God

When a believer re-enters a right relationship with God, everyone sees it. It's in his eyes; in his speech; in his purposes. A person in a right relationship with God is consumed with God. It reminds one of the Hymn, "Turn Your Eyes Upon Jesus":

> Turn your eyes upon Jesus,
> Look full in His wonderful face,
> And the things of this world will grow strangely dim,
> In the light of His glory and grace.

How true this is! When we keep our eyes and hearts on our Master, we are focused on "One Thing Needful". Look at the following passage from the Gospel of Luke and see the difference between the focus of two sisters by the names of Martha and Mary:

"Now it came to pass, as they went, that he entered into a certain village: and a certain woman named Martha received him into her house. And she had a sister called Mary, which also sat at Jesus' feet, and heard his word. But Martha was cumbered about much serving, and came to him, and said, Lord, dost thou not care that my sister hath left me to serve alone? bid her therefore that she help me. And Jesus answered and said unto her, Martha, Martha, thou art careful and troubled about many things: But one thing is needful: and Mary hath chosen that good part, which shall not be taken away from her" (Luke 10:38-42).

There is a vast lesson to be learned by all Christians and that is: **worship precedes service.** Martha was focused on service.

Nothing sinful about that. She had a desire to **serve** Jesus. Many of us have that desire. But her desire to serve was put before her desire to sit at His feet and worship and learn from Him. Her sister Mary knew *"the one thing needful."* Do we neglect God through service? Think about that. Is it possible to serve Him actively and still miss Him? How can this be? We must learn the lesson laid out for us in this passage of Scripture. Martha is focused on the wrong thing. Mary is focused on the right thing. It is not so much the **order** here as it is the **object.** If the object (in this case Jesus) is replaced by another object (in this case preparing a meal for fourteen people—the eleven disciples and the two sisters; Lazarus is not mentioned so we must assume he was away) then the **order** becomes out of focus. In other words, when our attention is first and foremost on **serving God** rather than **sitting at His feet,** we get things out of order and perform service without the anointing from above. It is far better to first get in the presence of God, stay there, tarry there, saturate ourselves with Him, then go out in service and do so in power! Did not Jesus say to the disciples to *"tarry ye in the city of Jerusalem"* for the Comforter? Why do we go out in service without first doing the same?

Would it not please God more if we first consult Him in prayer, find out what is on His heart and then go out in obedience to the King? It is interesting to note that the following chapter in the Gospel of Luke has to do with **prayer.** Do you think the Holy Spirit did this on purpose? Certainly! Notice the words of Jesus in the following verses, *"And I say unto you, Ask, and it shall be given you; seek, and ye shall find; knock, and it shall be opened unto you. For every one that asketh receiveth; and he that seeketh findeth; and to him that knocketh it shall be opened"* (Luke 11:9-10).

The Bible is there as a lesson book for us to follow as well as picture book for us to see Jesus. Do we apply what we read? Or are we like the person James describes? *"For if any be a hearer of the word, and not a doer, he is like unto a man beholding his natural face in a glass: For he beholdeth himself, and goeth his way, and straightway forgetteth what manner of man he was"* (Jas. 1:22-24).

A person on fire for God wants to stay in His presence. In Scripture, God is likened to fire—a wall of fire, a burning bush, a refiner's fire, eyes like fire etc. At the day of Pentecost, it was a symbol of fire that hung over the heads of the people in the person of the Holy Spirit. God is a consuming fire! Unfruitful vines will be cast into the fire to be burned. God wants His people to keep the embers of their hearts aflame. If we fail to pursue God in a love-hot relationship, then the drift sets in and soon, before we even realize it, we are lukewarm again or worse, we have fallen into grievous sin and God's heart is broken over us. Look at the depiction of a people outside of the will of God:

"And my people are bent to backsliding from me: though they called them to the most High, none at all would exalt him. How shall I give thee up, Ephraim? how shall I deliver thee, Israel? how shall I make thee as Admah? how shall I set thee as Zeboim? mine heart is turned within me, my repentings are kindled together. I will not execute the fierceness of mine anger, I will not return to destroy Ephraim: for I am God, and not man; the Holy One in the midst of thee: and I will not enter into the city" (Hos. 11:7-9).

What God is saying in this text is, though He is vexed with the sin of His straying people, He still has mercy towards them. An earthly monarch would destroy a rebel without any compassion toward the traitor. But though a straying people in their rebellion toward God deserve wrath, He grants mercy for He is not man but God! When God says, *"mine heart is turned within me"* this literally means "churned". If you have ever experienced a broken heart, you know the intensity of this feeling. God's pure heart breaks over our careless sin! When we get a larger view of God in His majesty, then we can see how He truly hates sin. His eyes cannot behold it! Why should we even tolerate it in our lives? This text is a clarion call to all believers to come back to God with a contrite heart in repentance and humility.

When we re-enter a right relationship with God, love pours from His big Father heart to ours and our hearts our filled with praise and worship toward Him! Some final thoughts will be seen in the following chapter on joy in the Lord.

*Dined at Old Ford, and gave a short exhortation to a
few people in a field, and preached, in the evening, at
a place called Mayfair, near Hyde Park Corner. The
congregation I believe, consisted of near eighty thousand people. It was, by far, the largest I ever preached
to yet. In the time of my prayer, there was a little
noise; but they kept a deep silence during my whole
discourse. A high and very commodious scaffold was
erected for me to stand upon; and though I was weak
in myself, yet God strengthened me to speak so loud,
that most could hear, and so powerfully, that most,
I believe, could feel. All love, all glory be to God
through Christ!*

George Whitefield

AFTERWORD:
Joy and Thanksgiving
in the Lord

A sign of a backslider is unhappiness and dissatisfaction in life. A grumbler is a backslider. A constant complainer is a backslider. I recently heard a minister preach in a little country church in the South and he said these words: "I have been in very poor health this last year, in fact many do not know how bad my health really is. And a year ago if you asked me how I was doing I would have taken an hour to tell you how bad I was doing. But God told me not to do this anymore. God told me that when someone asks me how I am doing I am to say, 'Fine. I am doing just fine!' And you know what, I have a peace and joy about that even in my trials."

It is easy to focus on ourselves in bad times. Either health problems or wealth problems or domestic problems can drag us down until we have a pity party for ourselves. Unfortunately the complaining eventually directs itself heavenward. We begin to doubt God's ability to help or even to hear our troubles. This is a signal of backsliding. When we fail to honour God, no matter what the circumstance we are providentially put in, we backslide. Our hearts begin to drift.

A believer who has learned to praise God even during trial brings glory to His name. Life can sometimes take away our happiness but no one can steal our joy in the Lord. The apostle Paul in prison, sitting in chains and cold, was able to say, *"Rejoice in the Lord always: and again I say, Rejoice"* (Phil. 4:4). There is a story told by J. Sidlow Baxter which bears telling here. Dr. Baxter was ill with an ear problem which made him have a constant noise in his ears. It became so distracting and annoying that his peace with God was disturbed and he began to complain about it more and more to those around him. The physical disorder was so unnerving it was beginning to disturb his joy and his peace in the Lord. Here is his telling of the incident:

> "Here's an experience which I recently had and which made this text unspeakably more precious to me (Philippians 4:6&7). It says you know if we commit everything to God by prayer and supplication with thanksgiving the peace of God shall guard our heart and minds. Have you ever thought about the peace of God? He had no beginnings. He has no end. He never changes. He has no equal. He has no superior. His plans never go wrong. None can thwart Him. He has no enemies but those He can obliterate whenever it pleases Him. His eternity has no disturbance. His infinity has no shadows. We fluctuating transient little mortals simply cannot imagine a peace like that. That's why the text says the peace of God that passes ALL imaginings. We would have said that such an experience of having that peace would be quite impossible except that God promises it. The peace of God shall guard your hearts and minds in Christ Jesus.

> "Let me close by relating this experience which I have referred to. At the time I was over in Scotland and at one point while there I slumped into a deep despondency. Everything seemed upsetting and frustrating and foreboding. There had been several acute trials and keen disappointments, and certain persons dear to me, for whose salvation I had prayed for over forty years, were seemingly as alienated from God as ever. It seemed as though the promises of the Bible were like pie crust. Was it any use praying longer? I was having trouble with deafness. And along with that, tinnitus, loud noises in both my ears day and night incessantly, almost dementing.

"A few days after that I had to preach morning and evening at the largest church in that area. And the prospect of it with my ear disability greatly upset me. And a few days after that preaching appointment I had to address ALL the ministers in that area. And the thought of that, with my double ear trouble and other things, almost had me out for the count. Do you know what that means? Out for the count? That's how I felt at the time.

"I was nervy, bitterly disappointed, deeply discouraged, and I went to bed weary with mental wrestling and frustration. And then, somewhere between night and morning, September 6th and 7th, something happened that changed everything. I heard no audible voice but someone had wakened me amid the curtains of the night; and was speaking within me. By a language which I knew at once. He said, 'Sid! Sid! Are you forgetting Philippians 4: verses 6 and 7? Those verses six and seven perfectly match September six and seven. You've been forgetting the thanksgiving. Hand everything over to Me Sid. And start praying again with thanksgiving. And start believing that what you ask for becomes yours. TRY IT Sid. And if you do Philippians 4:6 and 7 is all yours.'

"Well, I can't explain it too coherently but that is just what I did. In bed, there and then, amid the nocturnal darkness I handed everything over to Him. And I started praying again with thanksgiving. Somehow I did it with ease and then suddenly Philippians 4:6 and 7 was like an electric bulb turned on. And I saw everything with illuminating difference and clearness. My mental tension and gloom had gone. My anxiety had dropped away like a broken fetter. I felt renewed and so indeed I was. Soon after, I jumped out of bed and went downstairs for my time of early-morning prayer. And it was then that I began to realize something else. My hearing was better! I could hear everything now distinctly. And the ear noises had gone—completely. My whole nervous system had become relaxed. And as I prayed with thanksgiving—I could never forget it—the peace of God invaded my heart like a gentle zephyr. Or some halcyon calm. God had put a new song in my mouth." [11]

What Dr. Baxter realized was that through his illness and troubles he had unwittingly began a drift away from the promises of God. It is easy to backslide even if the individual is a much-used servant of God. The enemy of our souls will do all he can to disturb our peace and work havoc on our relationship with the Father! This often can be the case with an acute illness. Because of the physical discomfort and discouragement that accompanies such an illness, it is easy to give excuses for not rising early to have a daily "tryst" with the Lord. Anytime we move away from pursuing the presence of God in our lives it has deadly repercussions! The devil loves to sideline us from a prayer time with God. But we must fight for our "quiet time" for it is the most important area of our life!

This story from J. Sidlow Baxter highlights the drift that can transpire between God and a believer when there is an acute illness to deal with. It also provides the solution-prayer and thankfulness unto God! Having touched on the "thanksgiving" aspect of a fresh encounter with God we will now focus our attention on the "joy" aspect of such an encounter. Have you ever found it delightful to be around new believers? Their enthusiasm for the Lord is contagious! They have yet to allow their "first love" diminish like the rest of us. The following is a delightful story about a new convert who was brought to the Lord under the preaching of the Grand Itinerant of the Great Awakening, George Whitefield. This young girl wrote a letter to George Whitefield which was published in the "The Weekly History" of 1741. Here it is in its entirety:

> **From M. Finlysom, a young girl, to the Rev. Mr. Whitefield.**
> *"Much honoured and dearly beloved in our Lord*, Edinburgh Nov. 18, 1741.

---

11   E. A. Johnston, A Heart Awake: The Authorized Biography of J. Sidlow Baxter. (Grand Rapids: Baker Books, 2005) 124-126.

"I have taken this opportunity to write to you. My Heart is so full of Love to precious Christ, that I know not how to begin. O but I cannot forbear telling you how wonderfully my Lord has been dealing with my Soul since you left *Edinburgh*! O his Ways with my Soul have been all Wonders! O blessed, ever blessed, be the Hour that ever he was pleas' d to send you to this Place: For I am sure you was sent by the Lord to build me up and confirm me in the Ways of God. Before you came here I was doubtful of my eternal Salvation, but now I can say from sweet Experience, that I have not been this Quarter of a Year in the least Cloud about my Interest in Christ, I have just liv'd a Heaven upon Earth. O I have never experienced so much of his Presence as I have found when I have been hearing you preach. Indeed I may call the Park [Orphan House Park in Edinburgh] a *Bethel*; for surely God was in it many a Time. Every day I am getting a Sight of the Emptiness of myself, and the Fulness(sic) that is in precious Christ. O I see him to be full of Grace, full of Truth, full of Glory! I see him to be altogether lovely, white and ruddy, the Chief among ten Thousand. O I see him to be All in All! He is the only Desire of my Soul. O when I think upon the matchless Love of Christ. I am almost drown'd in a Sea of Wonders! O I wish I had ten thousand Times ten thousand Tongues to praise Him for that unmerited, unparelall'd(sic) Love unto the like of poor wretched, worthless, unworthy me. O praise be unto him for his Grace! Every day I receive more and more out of his Fullness. O I think that I can read my Interest in Christ as if it were written in Letters of Gold. O dear Sir, I think I never had such a Night in all the Days of my Life as I had that Night before you left *Edinburgh*: That Night I was taken up into Mount *Pisgah*, and I got a view of the Land that is afar off: That Night my Soul was fill'd with Joy unspeakable and glorious, I think I never enjoyed the like before. I went to Prayer and there I got near Access to the Throne of Grace, and there I got seal' d Pardon of all my Sins, he sent home that Word to my Mind, *Be of good Cheer, thy Sins are forgiven thee*. There I entered into Covenant with Him, and took Heaven and Earth to witness, I took Men and Angels to witness, I took Sun, Moon and Stars to witness that I was willing to accept of Christ, in all his Offices, as Prophet, Priest and King, and that if it were his Will to call me, I was willing to lay down my Life for his sake. That was a Night never to be forgotten by me. Indeed it is better felt than told. His Countenance shined so bright upon me that I just thought I was in Heaven: It was Heaven begun in my Soul indeed. And he set home that Word to my Mind, *I will make you complete in him*, who has Dominion over Principalities and Powers. And also that Word did comfort my Soul, *Ye are justified, ye are sanctified, by the Lord Jesus Christ, and by the Spirit of our God.* And the thirty first Day of October, it being Saturday, before the Communion Sabbath, I think was a great Day to my Soul indeed. I resolved to go up to the Table: My Heart was inflamed with Love to my dear Redeemer, that I was made willing to suffer any thing for Him, that ever was or could be invented. I was help'd to act Faith on the Son of God. All the Grace of the Holy Spirit was put into lively Exercise. O, I never got such a Sight of crucified Redeemer as I got that Day. I thought I saw him bleeding O the accursed Tree; and I thought I saw a Crown of Thorns upon his blessed Head. There, by Faith, I view'd him in the Garden sweating great Drops of Blood, and by Faith I view'd him drinking up the Dreggs of the Cup of his Father's Wrath. And I view'd those heart-killing Sins of mine that nailed my blessed Redeemer to the accursed Tree. I was filled with a Sense of his wonderful Love, and I was made to cry out with *Thomas*, MY LORD AND MY GOD! O dear Mr. *Whitefield*; I cannot express to you the joy that I felt in my Soul. I was so fill'd with the Love of precious and lovely Jesus, that I thought I would never fear what either Men or Devils would do unto me; I came up from the Table of the Lord making mention of his Righteousness, even of his only, saying *Only in the Lord Jesus have I Righteousness and Strength.* And I resolved, though he would slay me, yet I wou'd still trust in him. I was crying out with the Psalmist, *Through my Servant I shall never go back, nor turn from thee.* I resolved through his strength, that though all the Devils in Hell were roaring on me to go back, yet I wou'd not go back; but I wou'd continue stedfast(sic) in the Lord, and the Power of his Might. And ever since he hath ben(sic) daily loading me with his Benefits. O what shall I render to the Lord for all his Benefits towards me. O help me to praise Him, Men and Angels, Sun, Moon and Stars, come and help me to praise the Lord for his Wonders done towards me. O the matchless Love of Christ: that passeth all Knowledge. O! *Neither Death nor Life, nor Things present, nor Things to come, shall ever be able to separate me from the Love of God that is in Christ Jesus, my Lord I count all Things but Loss and Dung, for the Excellency of Christ Jesus, my Lord.* He hath promised that all is mine, and I am Christ's, and Christ is God's. O! Was there ever such condescending, wonderful Love, as this amazing Love of my dearest Saviour. O Glory, Glory be to his great Name for the Assurance that he has given me."[12]

Would it be so with each of us to have such a warm heart toward God! When a believer encounters God there is nothing else like it. We must each ask ourselves if our religion is intellectual or experiential. Are our hearts stirred within us toward spiritual things? If not we are either not truly born again believers or we are backsliders. Jesus did not come to die on a cross for people to remain indifferent or cold toward Him. He died to save us from our sins and He died to save us from the power of sin. As believers we will one day in the future be saved from the presence of sin with God in eternity! Let our time here on this earth be well spent for Him; let our hearts be on fire for Him; and let our lives be vessels in His Hand to be used by Him and for His glory! Be joyful in the Lord!

---

12   J. Lewis, *The Weekly History*, 312-314.

NO
TURNING BACK

Following Jesus Along the Narrow Way

The road to discipleship is a narrow one few follow, yet this is the road where Jesus is. If we are to be true disciples in following Him, we then must realign our lives and readjust our steps as we move upon that pathway where He leads. The road is not easy. The path is often challenging and hard. But the rewards are everlasting! In NO TURNING BACK, the author takes us on a road which leaves the mundane path of serving-self and introduces us to a selfless journey of following Christ. Once we begin this adventure and follow in the footsteps of the Master, there is NO TURNING BACK.

Binding: Paper
Size: 5.0" X 8.0"
Page Count: 120 pages
Item #: B-7221
ISBN : 1-897117-22-1
Genre: Christian Living

E. A. Johnston

GOSPEL FOLIO PRESS
I WILL PUBLISH THE NAME OF THE LORD

304 Killaly St. West | Port Colborne | ON | L3K 6A6 | Canada | 1 800 952 2382 | E-mail: info@gospelfolio.com | www.gospelfolio.com

Realities of
REVIVAL

"The short, but succinct, chapters of this book — THE REALITIES OF REVIVAL, are thought-provoking, heart searching, and will-bending...the sovereign work of God and the responsibility of man in revival are beautifully balanced and blended...Don't put the book down until you have read the last page!"

—from the Foreword
By Dr. Stephen F. Olford

Binding: Realities of Revival
Size: 5.0" X 8.0"
Page Count: 152 pages
Item #: B-7191
ISBN: 1-897117-19-1
Genre: Christian Growth

E. A. Johnston

GOSPEL FOLIO PRESS
I WILL PUBLISH THE NAME OF THE LORD

304 Killaly St. West | Port Colborne | ON | L3K 6A6 | Canada | 1 800 952 2382 | E-mail: info@gospelfolio.com | www.gospelfolio.com

KNOW THE BOOK
| Bible Survey At A Glance

Know The Book: Bible Survey At A Glance is a survey of each book of the Bible. At a glance the reader can grasp the central truths and content of each book. It is a helpful extra tool that can assist the reader:

- . Prepare Messages
- . Aid in Bible Studies
- . Teach Sunday School Classes

Know The Book: Bible Survey At A Glance will help you understand the history and time period of each book of the Bible at a glance. Difficult words (places and names) are pronounced for you. A practical application is presented with each book for today's Christian believer.

It is our desire that this research tool will enable the reader to be more knowledgeable, be more interesting, and be more effective in teaching, preaching and in the study of the Word of God. May God bless you as you handle His Holy Word!

Binding: Paper
Size: 6.0" X 9.0 "
Page Count: 148 pages
Item #: B-7337
ISBN : 1-897117-33-7
Genre: Bible Study

E. A. Johnston

GOSPEL FOLIO PRESS
I WILL PUBLISH THE NAME OF THE LORD

304 Killaly St. West | Port Colborne | ON | L3K 6A6 | Canada | 1 800 952 2382 | E-mail: info@gospelfolio.com | www.gospelfolio.com

TRUE DISCIPLESHIP

with Study Guide

Am I ignitable?

A disciple can be forgiven if he does not have great mental ability or physical prowess. But he cannot be excused if he does not have zeal. If his heart is not aflame with a red-hot passion for the Saviour, he stands condemned. After all, Christians are followers of the One who said, *"Zeal for Your house has eaten Me up"* (John 2:17). Their Saviour was consumed with a passion for God and for his interests. Those who are constrained b the love of Christ will count no sacrifice to great to make for him.

Binding: **Paper**
Size: **8.0" X 5.25"**
Page Count: **208 pages**
Item #: **B-1917**
ISBN : **1-882701-91-7**
Genre: **Christian Living**

William MacDonald

GOSPEL FOLIO PRESS

I WILL PUBLISH THE NAME OF THE LORD

304 Killaly St. West | Port Colborne | ON | L3K 6A6 | Canada | 1 800 952 2382 | E-mail: info@gospelfolio.com | www.gospelfolio.com

Printed in the United Kingdom
by Lightning Source UK Ltd.
124140UK00001B/91-120/A